ENVIRONMENT AND THE WORLD OF WORK

Report of the Director-General
of the International Labour Office
to the International Labour
Conference, 1990

International Labour Office, Geneva

Environment and the world of work, Report of the Director-General of the International Labour Office to the International Labour Conference, 1990
Geneva, International Labour Office, 1992

/Conference paper/, /Environmental protection/, /Environment/, /Employment/, /Work environment/, /Economic and social development/, /Role of ILO/. 16.03.4
ISBN 92-2-107114-6

ILO Cataloguing in Publication Data

Printed by the International Labour Office, Geneva, Switzerland

PREFACE

The dangers facing the environment are being discussed on all sides: in every speech, in every newspaper; and the threat is indeed a serious one. Sometimes it takes the ominous form of pollution and the depletion of natural resources. It thrives on appeasement. It knows no frontiers, respects no neutrality, affords no refuge. For the most pessimistic amongst us, it spells the end of the world unless we master it.

Rather than being prophets of doom, however, let us identify and evaluate all the means of warding off the danger, realistically and methodically.

We must all wage the fight together. The ILO in particular has an obvious mandate in its own field—and on two accounts.

Firstly, is not much of the damage to the environment created by our industrial society, by production, by labour? So although the Organisation is not involved with physical realities such as global warming, clean water or biological diversity, it has a clear duty to study the implications for the working world of measures taken to protect the environment. To be more precise, it must study their effects on employment and incomes, on the development of human resources and on the quality of conditions of work and life. I should like to emphasise the extent to which, throughout this Report, the analysis of the links between environment and work reflects the major concerns of the Organisation: protection of the working environment, the importance of training, the need for everyone to be made aware of his or her responsibilities, the need, too, for dialogue on these issues between the social partners, leading to consensus. Going to the heart of the matter, it is a question of the dignity of work.

But though everyone, or nearly everyone, agrees on general—and generous—principles, the actual implementation of effective environmental protection is another matter. For the political, economic, social and cultural realities must not be forgotten. Some of these realities are harsh indeed. Choices, sacrifices, are inevitable. Most populations of the North have enjoyed steadily rising improvements in the material quality of life for several decades, with little regard for the ecological cost. While one may welcome signs that part of the younger generation has rejected excessive consumerism, it is questionable to what extent these societies, as a whole, will voluntarily accept a change in life-style entailing a drop in living standards. Politicians are in a tight corner here, for societies are voters.

More specifically, in the field with which we are concerned, the head of an enterprise may be faced with the choice between maintaining maximum productivity in a particular branch of activity and accepting an increase in costs as a result of the elimination of toxic substances. This may well be an exaggeration and a simplification from the scientific point of view, but this is how the situation is seen by certain employers or certain occupational bodies. In many respects, in fact, it boils down to the question: who is going to pay for protecting our environment?

There is a second account on which the ILO has competence in respect of the environment, for paradoxically non-production, lack of work and extreme poverty in the Third World also give rise to problems of an ecological nature. The defence of the environment here puts a sharper edge on the dictum in the Declaration of Philadelphia that "poverty anywhere constitutes a danger to prosperity everywhere" and indeed on the whole approach of the ILO's Constitution. In many ways poverty is the most extreme form of pollution and a scourge that many developing countries cannot overcome by themselves. They cannot hope to make any headway without concerted support from the industrially developed countries.

This brings us back to the question: who is going to pay? Everyone agrees today that international co-operation is indispensable. But those responsible are less so when it comes to examining—not only within national societies but also between nations—the social and human implications of sharing the costs and benefits that result from environmental actions. Despite the fairly ready convergence of opinion concerning a common—even global—objective of safeguarding the environment, there are no simple, inexpensive solutions leading to that objective. Rather is there a danger of division, injustice and poverty being accentuated. This shows how closely the issue is bound up with the imperatives of economic and social justice. This shows, too, were it necessary, the need for environmental programmes to be integrated within overall policies for the improvement of conditions of work and life for all.

These are the considerations that must be borne in mind when reading this Report.

The ILO's Members are all concerned.

Governments, with their ministers of labour and employment, need to confront the economic and social ramifications of environmental problems and to bring their influence to bear accordingly on the relevant decision-making. As politicians, they will have to respond to the feelings and pressure of electorates for whom the ecology is no longer merely a fashionable conversation piece but is becoming a rallying point, a current of growing strength in their country's mainstream politics.

Employers and managers have to face a daunting double challenge: to develop and apply new environmentally "clean" technologies and processes while generating the economic growth to help foot the bill.

For workers and their organisations there is the need to show solidarity with their fellow workers throughout the world who are affected by these problems and policies, and to press for protective measures which share equitably the burden and the benefit of environmental action.

Here and throughout the working world the imperative is dialogue between the three groups to achieve consensus.

At global level, the structure for this dialogue exists already within our Organisation. It remains for the ILO to define its role in the environmental field and to fine-tune its instruments of action accordingly. My Report raises more questions than it offers solutions. It does, however, point the way to solutions. But I look to the discussion on this paper for more specific guidance.

The Report proposes a series of initiatives. The first, most obvious one, is to encourage tripartism on this issue too: not only to make the fullest use of it within the ILO—which is the only way of achieving realistic results—but also to promote its use among the ILO's constituents, wherever it can appropriately apply. If any issue calls for the creative dynamism of meaningful popular participation, it is precisely this one.

The second initiative consists in defining the ways and means of standard-setting activity so as to influence national policy and practice. The third aims at integrating ecological considerations into technical co-operation activities and indeed into all activities where they can bear fruit; in particular, this means establishing at a practical level the relationship between the working environment and the general environment, which I see as a basic concept. Overall, I propose that the ILO should co-operate to the maximum in the efforts of the United Nations system to secure a global, interdisciplinary approach to environmental action—action which incorporates and reflects the economic, social or simply human implications I have mentioned.

The issue of the environment is vast and difficult. Obviously, the ILO cannot do everything. Nor can it be expected to. But it has its share of responsibility in the management of natural and human resources and must do everything within its power to accomplish its task as effectively as possible. It is my hope, in presenting this Report to the Conference, that a clear recognition will emerge of the responsibility we all share within the ILO for a situation which concerns us all, and of the need for immediate and long-term measures to deal with it on a universal, interdependent basis. I trust that in this way we shall be able to take realistic and equitable action in harmony with the Organisation's great human tradition.

23 February 1990   Michel HANSENNE

CONTENTS

INTRODUCTION

ENVIRONMENT AND DEVELOPMENT AND THE ILO

The decade of the 1980s has closed to a crescendo of conferences, meetings, reports and statements drawing attention to a vast and varied agenda of environmental issues confronting our planet. The response to the concerns and conclusions of the report of the World Commission on Environment and Development entitled *Our common future* (known as the Brundtland Report), to the accelerating series of environmental accidents such as Seveso, Bhopal, Chernobyl, Schweizerhalle and Exxon Valdez, as well as to greater scientific knowledge and increased public awareness of issues such as ozone depletion and global warming, has been to place environment at the top of the political agenda in many countries, as well as internationally.

Although numerous national, regional and international conventions and protocols have been concluded as a result of this growing awareness and commitment, they may be only the tip of an iceberg of regulatory activities in the 1990s.

In the ILO, the environment has rightly been claiming increasing attention. For several years now, a number of resolutions on the subject have been brought before the Resolutions Committee of the Conference but have never had the opportunity to be fully examined. The wide level of interest in the environment expressed at recent sessions of the Conference, however, suggests that the time is now ripe for a more formal discussion of these important issues by the Conference.

The Fourth European Regional Conference (1987) and the Seventh African Regional Conference (1988) have already adopted resolutions concerning the environment. In late 1989, the ILO convened a special Tripartite Meeting of Experts on Employment and Training Implications of Environmental Policies in Europe, which adopted a number of conclusions on these questions. Furthermore, several Industrial Committees and tripartite technical meetings have adopted resolutions concerning environmental matters within their specific sectors, viz., chemicals, iron and steel, coal mining, petroleum, fishing, etc.

The ILO has been actively concerned with environmental questions since 1919, although until recently most of our activities have been focused on the working environment. Nevertheless, for the past 20 years our activities related to the general environment have been expanding and include training, technical co-operation and research. I have attached as an Annex to this Report the report on Environmentally Sound and Sustainable Development, submitted by the Governing Body to the 44th Session of the United Nations General Assembly, which provides a detailed review of our past, present and possible future activities concerning the environment and development.

I should also note, however, that this subject is not a new one for the International Labour Conference. Eighteen years ago, at the 57th Session of the Conférence in 1972, the title of the Director-General's Report was *Technology for freedom: Man in his environment—The ILO contribution.* That Report stated:

We cannot turn our backs on economic growth and technological innovation on the ground that they are responsible for the deterioration of the environment. Economic growth is the motive power of development, . . . there is no irreconcilable conflict between growth and innovation and environmental protection. We need increased productivity to provide the wherewithal for improving and protecting the environment. This is particularly true in the developing countries, where many of the most serious environmental problems are linked directly to poverty (p. 9).

In 1972 the Conference adopted a resolution concerning the contribution of the International Labour Organisation to the protection and enhancement of the environment related to work, which pledged the full support and effective action of the International Labour Organisation to any concerted world campaign for the protection and enhancement of the human environment. I have attached the full text of the resolution as an Annex, as it gives an interesting perspective on how the international community's concern for the environment has changed but also how it has remained relevant to today's environmental agenda.

When I read the 1972 resolution during the preparation of this Report, I became even more convinced that the ILO's constituents and the Organisation and Office should play a more active role in the major environmental efforts of the 1990s and beyond.

The environmental issues and policies which will be discussed in this Report are mainly those which have a potential impact on the world of work, i.e. the common concerns of the ILO's constituents, which is far greater than is now realised. Unlike several decades ago, the concept of the environment has considerably evolved from a narrow focus on pollution to cover the management of environmental resources necessary for development; in other words, it now entails an integrated approach to environment and development.

This change in perspective has resulted largely from the efforts of the United Nations Environment Programme (UNEP) and its Executive Director, Dr. M. Tolba, and from the work of the World Commission on Environment and Development (WCED) chaired by Dr. Gro Harlem Brundtland. In 1987 both UNEP's *Environmental perspective to the year 2000 and beyond* and the WCED's report, *Our common future* (Brundtland Report) were published and examined by the General Assembly of the United Nations. Together these two key documents have fueled a growing debate and have inspired measures involving a series of actions concerning new approaches to environment and development for the decades to come. The Brundtland Report exposes the error of the past approach to environment and development which pursued separate and competing objectives and pleads for an integrated approach in development policies and projects which, if environmentally sound, will lead to sustainable development in both developed and developing countries. It emphasises the need to give higher priority to anticipatory and preventive policies, in addition to correcting immediate environmental problems. In the words of the WCED: "sustainable development is development that meets the needs of the present without compromising the ability of future generations to meet their own needs".

It emphasises the concept of needs, in particular the essential needs of the world's poor, to which overriding priority should be given, as well as recalling the limitations imposed by the state of technology and describes national and international institutional arrangements to meet present and future environment and development objectives.

A vital component of the concept of sustainable development is that environmental challenges cannot be met without at the same time meeting basic social and economic development objectives. This parallels the ILO's own proposition expressed in the Declaration of Philadelphia that "poverty anywhere constitutes a danger to prosperity everywhere". In addition, the ILO's fundamental principle that "lasting peace can be established only if it is based on social justice" is also directly related to many of the fundamental environmental challenges of today. Without an equitable sharing of the costs and benefits of environmental protection within and between countries, neither social justice nor sustainable development can be achieved. As His Holiness Pope John Paul II stated in his message celebrating the World Day of Peace on 1 January 1990: "In our day, there is a growing awareness that world peace is threatened not only by the arms race, regional conflicts and continued injustices among people and nations, but also by a lack of due respect for nature, by the plundering of natural resources and by a progressive decline in the quality of life." The issue of the environment today and in the decades ahead may indeed significantly influence the achievement of the ILO's own basic objectives.

The Brundtland Report notes that the pursuit of sustainable development requires:

— a *political system* that secures effective citizen participation in decision-making,
— an *economic system* that is able to generate surpluses and technical knowledge on a self-reliant and sustained basis,
— a *social system* that provides for solutions for the tensions arising from disharmonious development,
— a *production system* that respects the obligation to preserve the ecological base for development,
— a *technological system* that can search continuously for new solutions,
— an *international system* that fosters sustainable patterns of trade and finance, and
— an *administrative system* that is flexible and has the capacity for self-correction.

The ILO's tripartite constituents play an active role in every one of the above-cited systems and, therefore, have an opportunity to influence the achievement of sustainable development.

One of the most important conclusions reached during the preparation of the present Report was that the main difficulties in dealing with the environment are not technical, but political, economic and social. The problems lie in the lack of political will or institutional capacity; the lack of adequate financial resources or unwillingness to devote adequate financial resources to environmental objectives; and the conflicts, divisions, diversity and disparity within our societies which prevent us from reaching consensus on what to do, how to do it and how to pay for it.

When one looks at the environment from these perspectives, the role of the ILO's constituents, particularly the employers and workers, in helping to achieve a constructive consensus on the environment both internationally and within their national societies could be very significant—if not indeed a prerequisite for success.

One of the goals of this Report, therefore, is to identify possible ways in which governments, especially ministries of labour and employment, and employers' and workers' organisations can promote and participate in environmentally sound and sustainable development. In order to play such a role, however, the ILO's tripartite constituents need to be aware of the potentially negative and positive repercussions—or the costs and benefits—of environmental policies upon the world of work. So far little attention has been given to the analysis of such repercussions and this has made the preparation of this Report difficult. Despite such constraints, however, the ILO's constituents need to consider these questions now and not later.

The Report has three main objectives. First, to increase the environmental awareness of delegates attending the International Labour Conference, particularly as regards the potential implications of environmental problems and policies for traditional labour and social issues of concern to the ILO. Second, it seeks to identify a number of environmental issues and policy areas currently being discussed in various national, regional and international forums which may warrant more active attention and action by the ILO's tripartite constituents. Third, it indicates a number of possible priorities calling for direct action by the International Labour Organisation and Office.

To achieve these objectives, the Report has been structured as follows: Chapter 1 provides an overview of environment and development issues including those related to land and its living resources, water resources and the atmosphere. A brief discussion of several important national and international issues of environmental policy is presented in Chapter 2. Chapter 3 focuses the potential impact of environmental problems and policies on the world of work, especially employment, poverty and development, training, the working environment and industrial relations. The role of the ILO's tripartite constituents is examined in Chapter 4 and that of the International Labour Organisation and Office is discussed in Chapter 5.

OVERVIEW OF ENVIRONMENTAL AND DEVELOPMENT ISSUES

1

Before examining the specific effects of environmental and development issues on the world of work, it may be useful to provide an overview of some of the most important challenges confronting us. One of these—the rapid growth in world population—is having overwhelming implications for the quality of life and the environment.

While it took more than 100 years for the world's population to double from 1.25 billion to 2.5 billion in 1950, it doubled again in only 37 years, reaching 5 billion in 1987. The United Nations now projects that world population will exceed 6 billion by the year 2000 and more than 8 billion by the year 2025. It is further projected that population is likely to stabilise at about 10 billion towards the end of the next century.

This rapidly growing population will require more food, fuel, shelter, education and health care and increasing demands will consequently be made on the ILO and its tripartite constituents in respect of employment and income opportunities, safe working environments, social security and the protection of social justice. The provision of these essential needs, however, will dramatically increase pressure upon our natural resources and environment. This is even more apparent when one examines the present distribution of population and the disparate rates of population growth on our planet.

Between 1900 and 1950 the population of the developed countries represented approximately one-third of the world's population. By 1985, however, it had decreased to less than one-quarter. Furthermore, in view of the very substantial differences in age structure between developed and developing countries, this trend is likely to continue. Over 90 per cent of the projected additional 3 billion people in the year 2025 are likely to be in what are today classified as low-income countries in Africa, Asia and Latin America. These developing countries, whose natural resources are in many cases already suffering significant degradation and depletion, will need to achieve rapid economic growth if they are to meet even the very minimum requirements of their populations. However, this economic growth, so urgently needed to alleviate poverty, will have to be achieved without placing unsustainable pressures on local and global environmental resources.

Rapid urbanisation has been closely linked to the increase in population: in 1940 one person in eight lived in an urban area, in 1980 one in three, and it is now projected that by the year 2000 it will be one in two.[1] There will be 30 megacities (over 5 million) in developing countries by the year 2000 with a total population of approximately 330 million.[2] Furthermore, there has been a similar shift in the balance of poverty from rural to urban areas. The World Bank estimates that by the end of the 1990s, 90 per cent of the absolute poor in Latin America and the Caribbean will be living in cities, as will 40 per cent in Africa and 45 per cent in Asia.[3]

The growth of cities, particularly in developing countries, creates a "syphoning effect" which significantly influences the movement of food, fuels and other natural resources from surrounding areas, in turn affecting the environment and people in rural areas. In addition to the problem of growth, however, other cities, particularly in industrialised countries, are encountering problems of decay—loss of population and economic activities, and deteriorating housing, infrastructure and services. Furthermore, the disposal of urban solid wastes has become an urgent and costly problem for many cities around the world.

LAND AND ITS LIVING RESOURCES

Land degradation

In 1977 the United Nations Conference on Desertification defined desertification as "the diminution or destruction of the biological potential of the land" and focused the world's attention on the problems of drought and its effect on human welfare. This definition goes far beyond the encroachment of land by desert sands to include a much wider concept of land degradation caused by deforestation, accelerated soil erosion, and the water-logging and salinisation of once-productive irrigated lands. As land becomes degraded through over-grazing, mismanagement of the soil and water resources, and the exploitation of farm land beyond its capacity, the local people, who are often poor and without any alternative sources of livelihood, are trapped in a vicious cycle of poverty and environmental degradation. As more people struggle to gain their livelihood from the land, traditional patterns of shifting cultivation which permitted soils to recover have been abandoned. Furthermore, people are moving to increasingly marginal land or misusing land—as in the case of the "slash and burn" practice in tropical rain forests which cannot support crops on a sustainable basis.

In order to meet the food needs of the rapidly growing population, more intensive production will be required on existing land, large areas of which are already subject to degradation. It is likely, therefore, that degraded lands will need to be restored or rehabilitated if human needs are to be met in the next century. While such activities are expensive, the costs in human and economic terms of doing nothing will be much higher.

In addition to the billions of dollars lost due to declining agricultural productivity, there are many "unaccounted" social costs such as famine, disease, civil unrest and the massive dislocation of "environmental refugees". These environmental and social costs are most often borne by the rural poor, who live on marginal lands, but in time these costs will also affect entire nations. Despite the long-term bene-fits of action to protect or restore land, the subsistence farmers living in the shadow of famine and poverty will need help to make the necessary investments to secure their future—and that of the land.

Land recovery programmes will, however, entail labour-intensive activities which may provide a fresh impetus to employment creation, generating new income opportunities and helping to slow the rural-urban drift.

Deforestation

Forests and woodlands cover almost one-third of the world's land surface and constitute one of earth's main natural resources. They help to regulate our climate, protect water resources and also provide us with forest products worth almost US$100 billion per year.[4] Nevertheless, the world's forests are rapidly diminishing. Some 100 million people in 22 countries no longer have enough trees to meet even their minimum fuel requirements, and this makes life particularly hard for the poorer women of these countries, whether in urban or rural environments. Half of the world's population depends on forests for fuel and fodder. Every year between 10 and 20 million hectares of tropical forests and woodlands are destroyed and the inter-national community, through the United Nations system, is working to protect the tropical forests and manage them more efficiently by such means as the creation of a special Tropical Forestry Action Plan and the establishment of the International Tropical Timber Organisa-tion.

However, world-wide attention has been focused primarily on the rapid rate of deforestation for agricultural or other purposes, espe-cially in the Amazon, underlining the role of tropical forests as the "lungs of the planet" which may influence global warming through the release (when burned) and absorption (when growing) of carbon dioxide in the atmosphere. The main causes of deforestation have been the clearing of land for agriculture and cattle grazing to feed growing numbers of people or to earn urgently needed foreign exchange from exports of such commodities as soyabeans, cotton or coffee, and beef as well as timber. While some of the deforestation taking place has actually been planned and promoted by governments, a substantial proportion takes place spontaneously and without control.[5] Often this is the work of millions of landless people who have no alternative means of livelihood. One aspect of special concern to the ILO is the impact of deforestation upon forest populations, who include many millions of indigenous and tribal peoples who live in, or depend on, the forests for the continuation of their traditional way of life.

In addition to the threats to the forests referred to above, in Europe air pollution is suspected of having caused "moderate or severe damage" to almost 15 per cent of the total timber volume in 17 countries.[6] Such damage could mean that mountain communities risk losing their protection against avalanches and could increase the danger of flash floods and erosion; alternative protective measures would be expensive.

More attention will need to be given to the important economic benefits of maintaining forests. These benefits range from flood prevention and the protection of scarce clean water resources to employment in forest management, and include the harvesting of fruits, fodder, medicinal plants and special materials such as rubber. Nor should tourism be overlooked. The economic benefits of forests have too often been seen from a very short-term economic perspective which ignored environmental and longer-term socio-economic costs and benefits to the local population, country and climate.

Biological diversity

"Biological diversity is the wealth of life on earth, the millions of plants, animals and micro-organisms, the genes they contain and the intricate ecosystems they help build into the living environment."[7] Animal and plant species are becoming extinct at an unprecedented rate due to the global deterioration of the natural environment. This is particularly the case for ecosystems such as tropical forests, coral reefs and wetlands that are rich in species. The full biological diversity of this planet, however, is still unknown but may yield important discoveries that will help humanity to meet its future food, fuel, health and other requirements. In addition to such economic and social factors, there are also fundamental ethical considerations related to the protection of biological diversity that should be borne in mind in the future.

Although over 7,000 kinds of plants have been grown or collected for food throughout history, only a tiny fraction of species with potential economic importance have been used and today a mere 20 of them supply 90 per cent of the world's food. Biological diversity has had an important impact on the development of new medicines and also contributes to industry by providing such natural resources as rubber, natural starches, fats and oils and natural pesticides. While the importance of biological diversity to the world of work may seem remote, it may in fact provide important new breakthroughs, particularly by means of biotechnology, which will help to meet the growing requirements of the world's population.

WATER RESOURCES

Fresh water resources

Although over 70 per cent of the earth's surface is covered by water, 97 per cent of this is seawater and of the remaining 3 per cent of fresh water only 1 per cent is available for human use. Nevertheless, if it were managed efficiently, there would be enough water to meet human needs, both now and in the future.

Agriculture is the greatest user of fresh water (approximately 70 per cent), mostly for irrigation which is often inefficient and ineffective and can even lead to soil being waterlogged and salinised. Intensive agriculture based on chemical agents for fertilisers and crop protection in both developed and developing countries has also become a major cause of groundwater contamination by nitrates and pesticides. In addition, the run-off water from agricultural areas has led to serious pollution problems for rivers, coastal areas and seas.

Industry uses much less water (21 per cent) but has become a very important source of pollution. Most of the water in industry is used for cooling and cleaning and, although more than 80 per cent of it is returned to its source, it is often polluted with by-products from the industrial process and its temperature is sometimes increased, which can alter the ecological balance drownstream. Recently, growing attention has been given to the role of groundwater pollution, including the effects on drinking water, resulting from the unsafe disposal of chemical and other waste by industry. The OECD has described the vulnerability of groundwater to industrial and other forms of pollution as a "hidden time bomb".[8]

It is estimated that three-quarters of the Third World's rural population lack access to reasonably safe supplies of water and that almost 75 per cent of the population in developing countries lack adequate sanitary facilities. Most human waste is simply dumped in the nearest course of flowing water, with the result that human waste has become one of the world's most dangerous environmental pollutants. Four out of every five common diseases in developing countries are caused either by dirty water or lack of sanitation, and water-borne diseases alone cause an average of about 25,000 deaths a day in the Third World.[9]

In 1981 the United Nations launched the International Drinking Water Supply and Sanitation Decade with the objective of providing everyone with safe water and adequate sanitation by 1990. The investments needed to achieve that objective represent a very heavy burden for both developed and developing countries (UNEP estimated them at between US$300 and US$600 billion), but clean water and sanitation facilities are essential factors which must be integrated within overall development and environment plans, policies and programmes. In the future the problem of fresh water may also raise questions of economic and social justice as the poorest sections of the community, the people living downstream, are left with water supplies—upon which their livelihood and survival may depend—that are inadequate or polluted. The achievement of the objective for the Decade, which, despite major efforts, is still far away for most developing countries, is essential if the conditions of work and life of literally billions of people on this planet are to be improved.

The marine environment

The oceans cover over 70 per cent of the planet's surface and play a vital role in maintaining its life-support systems, moderating climate, and sustaining fish, animals and plants. They are an important source of protein and energy and play a leading role in the fields of transportation, employment and recreation as well as in other economic, social and cultural activities. They are also, however, the ultimate disposal site for the by-products of many human activities, receiving waste from cities, farms and industries via sewage outfalls, dumping from barges and ships, coastal run-off, river discharge and even airborne pollution. While public attention has tended to focus upon recent major accidents such as the Exxon Valdez oil spill in Alaska and the outbreaks of algal blooms in Scandinavia (1988) and the Adriatic Sea (1989), the day-to-day run-off from our industrial, agricultural and human settlement activities is having a much more profound effect upon coastal waters, regional seas and oceans.

Where the combined effects of over-fishing and pollution are leading to regional reductions in fish catches, the hardest hit may be artisanal fishermen and others in coastal areas of developing countries who depend heavily on fish for protein and on fishing for employment.[10] In its 1987 report on world fisheries, the FAO noted that "the time of spectacular and sustained increases in fisheries, catches is over."[11] The main reason cited for this reduction is over-fishing, "which has exceeded the regenerative capacity of the world's fish stocks".[12]

In response to the significant pollution caused by shipping and maritime activities, the International Maritime Organization has established a co-ordinated Strategy for the Protection of the Marine Environment to deal with the questions of pollution from ships and the disposal of waste at sea. Most attention has been focused on oil pollution, which has had significant adverse effects, including economic and employment losses for the local population and damage to wildlife and the natural environment. However, many of the chemicals carried by sea are far more dangerous to the marine environment. Many of these substances not only present a considerable threat of pollution but can also be extremely hazardous to personnel on board ship, to fishermen, and those involved in the loading and handling of such substances, as well as to coastal populations.[13]

Damage to maritime resources can have serious repercussions on the work of coastal communities, particularly fishermen, and on the related economic infrastructure, e.g. processing, transport and marketing. In addition, many coastal areas depend on tourism and fishing for their economic survival and, as has been learned following oil spills and algal blooms, such events can create enormous hardship.

THE ATMOSPHERE

Climate change and the greenhouse effect

The fact that the World Meteorological Organisation (WMO) and the United Nations Environment Programme (UNEP) have established an Intergovernmental Panel on Climate Change (IPCC) is just one of many examples of how world-wide attention has become focused on the issue of greenhouse gases and climate. It is a most complex issue and, although great efforts are being made by the international community to expand scientific knowledge, much remains uncertain—and sometimes controversial. Although it may at first appear unlikely that climate change could have implications for the ILO, both the potential effects of climate change and the possible policy responses to prevent or to delay it might well have a considerable impact on the world of work.

Without the natural greenhouse effect, life on earth would not be possible as surface temperatures would be too low. The atmosphere keeps us warm by absorbing heat—much like a greenhouse. The earth's temperature has remained relatively stable, despite some natural fluctuations, over the past few thousand years. Recently, however, the relatively small increases in the level of certain trace gases (for example carbon dioxide, nitrous oxide, methane, chlorofluorocarbons (CFCs) and ozone) resulting from human activities, particularly energy production, transportation, industry, agriculture and forestry, are threatening to disturb this natural cycle.

It is estimated that the global mean temperature may increase by between 1.5° C and 4.5° C by the year 2030.[14] Nevertheless, the magnitude and rate of this global warming, its regional distribution and its results remain the subject of widespread study and debate. For example, it is estimated that global warming of the magnitude cited above might lead to a sea level rise of 20 to 140 cm. Such rises in sea level could inundate low-lying areas, destroy coastal marshes and swamps, erode shore lines, worsen the coastal flooding effects of storms, and increase the salinity of coastal waters and bays. The effect of such sea level changes on the large number of people living in such areas throughout the world is hard to imagine, but none the less their likelihood is potentially very real.[15]

In addition, global warming affects regional climate and particularly precipitation levels. Higher latitudes may heat up more than equatorial regions which may alter wind and rainfall patterns. This could have an impact on many terrestial ecosystems, with implications for global vegetation, food production and its distribution.

Climate change is now at the forefront of today's environmental agenda. Already response strategies to limit carbon dioxide emissions are being considered which might entail considerable restructuring of the energy and transportation sectors of our economies. What would be the social reaction to strategies calling, for example, for major shifts in the present energy mix away from fossil fuels, introducing major energy conservation programmes or setting up new transport systems less reliant on cars—and what effect would they have on employment and the working environment? If indeed such major restructuring of the economy were required, how would governments, employers and workers cope with such change? Although these issues may seem remote, they are already being actively discussed by the Intergovernmental Panel on Climate Change (IPCC). Ministries of labour and employment and employers' and workers' organisations should examine how they might play a more active role in the process of defining such response strategies to future environmental problems.

Ozone depletion

One of the essential components of the atmosphere is a fragile natural filter of ozone which screens out almost all the harmful ultraviolet (UV) rays of the sun. The small amount of UV radiation that does penetrate the shield causes considerable harm, including human health problems such as some types of skin cancer, cataracts and weakening of the body's immune system. In addition to these effects upon humans, many crops and other plants are sensitive to present levels of UV radiation and any significant increase in the future could influence the productivity of agriculture and forestry. Similarly, UV radiation might also cause damage beneath the surface of the sea (in clean waters as deep as 20 metres), particularly to small creatures such as plankton, fish larvae, shrimps and crabs, and plants—all essential links in the food chain of the sea.

During the past 15 years, scientists have confirmed that the ozone layer is particularly threatened by a group of chemicals which when first discovered in the 1930s were considered "miracle" substances:

chlorofluorocarbons (CFCs). Their use has rapidly expanded as refrigerants, propellants, solvents and foaming agents which now play a critical role in many industrial and commercial activities.

The stability of CFCs, which makes them so useful on earth, however, also enables them to attack the ozone layer. While other substances also pose a threat to the ozone layer, none are so harmful as CFCs. Scientific research has now established that CFCs are responsible for the most dramatic evidence of ozone depletion, the so-called "hole" in the ozone layer which appears each southern spring over Antarctica. In addition, it is now generally accepted that ozone depletion is also taking place all over the world at an increasing rate.

This evidence alerted scientists and governments to one of the first truly global environmental problems. UNEP launched a project in 1975 to identify hazards threatening the ozone layer. This work culminated in the adoption, in Vienna in 1985, of the Convention for the Protection of the Ozone Layer which in 1987 was supplemented by the Montreal Protocol on Substances that Deplete the Ozone Layer. The latter provides special concessions for countries with small CFC industries, centrally planned economies and developing countries so as to ensure that such global provisions do not impinge inequitably upon their development. By the time the Protocol came into force in 1989, however, science had progressed to the point where even the limits it prescribes appeared insufficient in the light of the menace from CFCs. Furthermore, implementation of these instruments is likely to have important economic, employment and social consequences in both developed and developing countries which are discussed further on.

Air quality

Air pollution has for some time been a major local environmental problem in most countries, especially in urban and industrial areas. The causes are well known: the release of a wide range of air pollutants resulting from such common features of urban life as electricity generation, industrial processes, the burning of household fuels and vehicle emissions. One policy response to industrial pollution, introduced in the 1960s, was the construction of taller chimneys. While this helped to solve the immediate problem of local air pollution, it also set in process one of the major air pollution problems of the 1970s and 1980s—i.e. long-distance and transboundary effects, such as acid deposition (acid rain). As a result, what was once a local problem has increasingly assumed regional and international dimensions. It affects human health, agriculture, forest growth, water resources, fisheries and buildings and structures—and it is costly. The OECD estimated in 1985 that air pollution damage in France amounted to 1 per cent of the gross national product and in the Netherlands to 2 per cent.[16] Furthermore, efforts to decrease emissions of these pollutants are also expensive. For example, air pollution abatement expenditure on new plant and equipment for all manufacturing industries in the United States in 1987 amounted to $2.63 billion, or 1.8 per cent of total new manufacturing expenditure.[17]

While great progress has been made in reducing emissions, much still needs to be done, especially in the rapidly growing urban areas of developing countries. The World Health Organization (WHO) estimates that more than 1.2 billion people may be living in areas where airborne particulate matter exceeds WHO recommended limits.[18] The effect of deteriorating air quality for such large segments of the world population has and will continue to have negative implications for the world of work. If workers in their non-working hours are exposed to pollutants which affect their general health and conditions of life, this may have a direct effect on their health and productivity at work. Those who work out of doors (workers in the informal sector, transport and construction) are likely to be particularly affected by these general environmental conditions. Similarly, attention should also be given to the implication that the abatement and control of emissions from enterprises are likely to have on the working environment within those enterprises.

A wide range of international and regional agreements and national laws and regulations are aimed at limiting air pollution, particularly in industrialised countries. As these policies will probably need to be strengthened, it may be expected that increasing investments in air pollution abatement and control technologies, new "cleaner" industrial processes, and monitoring and control activities will be required. Such investments may lead to important employment implications, which will be discussed in more detail in Chapter 3.

Notes

[1] *Our common future*, report of the World Commission on Environment and Development (the Brundtland Report) (Oxford, OUP, 1987, p. 235.

[2] *World resources 1988-89*, report by the World Resources Institute and the International Institute for Environment and Development in collaboration with UNEP (Basic Books, New York, 1988), pp. 38-39.

[3] ibid., p. 37.

[4] *UNEP Profile* (Nairobi, May 1987), p. 12.

[5] *World resources 1988-89*, op. cit., p. 71.

[6] ibid., p. 76.

[7] WWF-World Wide Fund for Nature: *The importance of biological diversity* (Gland, Switzerland), p. 3.

[8] F. Juhasz: "Water: Is there a crisis?", in *The OECD Observer*, No. 160, Oct.-Nov. 1989, p. 5.

[9] *Safeguarding the world's water*, UNEP Environment Brief No. 6.

[10] *World resources 1988-89*, op. cit., p. 146.

[11] ibid., p. 147.

[12] *FAO and the environment* (FAO, Rome, 1986), p. 17.

[13] International Maritime Organization: *Strategy for the protection of the marine environment* (London, July 1988).

[14] UNEP: *The ozone layer*, UNEP/GEMS (Global Environment Monitoring System) Environment Library No. 2 (Nairobi, 1987), p. 6.

[15] *Climate change: Meeting the challenge*, report by a Commonwealth Group of Experts (Commonwealth Secretariat, London, Sep. 1989).

[16] UNEP: *1989: The state of the world environment* (Nairobi, 1989), p. 1.

[17] US Department of Commerce: *Survey of current business* (Washington, DC, Nov. 1988), p. 26.

[18] WHO and UNEP/GEMS: *Global pollution and healths*, results of health-related environmental monitoring, 1987, p. 7.

ENVIRONMENTAL POLICY ISSUES

2

The environment and development issues described in Chapter 1 have aroused rapidly growing public and political awareness and concern, which in turn have led to a wave of international, national and local discussions on environmental policy. This chapter gives a brief description of some of the policy issues likely to have a particularly significant impact on the world of work.

It should be noted, however, that there is in fact one central issue which pervades almost every environmental policy discussion—how to share equitably the costs and benefits of environmental action. "Who will pay for environmental improvements?" is a question which will need to be discussed and resolved at all levels, from the perspective of consumers, workers and employers, as well as from that of local, national, regional and international institutions.

For the ILO, the social and human implications of how these potential environmental costs and benefits are shared within society and between countries may be as important as the environmental actions themselves. An inequitable sharing of the social, economic and environmental costs and benefits of development, within and between countries, cannot lead to global sustainable development. Rather, it could accentuate poverty, injustice and division. Therefore, our search for environmental policies in the future should shift from a narrow and isolated approach focused on the environment to an integrated approach aimed at achieving economic, social and environmental objectives which are centred upon improving the quality of work and life for all.

THE "POLLUTER PAYS PRINCIPLE" VS. "THE SOCIETY PAYS PROBLEM"

The Brundtland Report places great emphasis on the importance of preventing environmental damage and pollution, rather than seeking remedies afterwards. Such an approach will be crucial for the successful achievement of sustainable development because most economic theories have tended to ignore or greatly underestimate the "externalities" or costs of pollutant emissions into the atmosphere, the oceans and the land (e.g. waste-disposal sites). As we approach, and in some cases already surpass, the capacity of our air, water and soil to absorb this pollution without being adversely affected, what were previously perceived as "cost-free disposal sites" are becoming very expensive charges on society. Despite the widespread endorsement of the "polluter pays principle", in practice this has too often become the "society pays problem". Shifting the economic burden onto society can have very inequitable effects on various segments of society, particularly the poor, the unemployed and retired workers. Such implications apply also to global environmental problems between countries, further complicating the search for equitable ways to share the costs of environmental protection.

The various "guesstimates" of the possible costs of adequate environmental protection and rehabilitation necessary to achieve sustainable development are indeed hard to imagine—ranging in the hundreds of billions, if not trillions, of US dollars. Since the Industrial Revolution began, industry and society have been abusing the environment by not paying its "environmental costs" on a regular basis, and in effect, mortgaging those costs into the future. However, *the future is now,* when it comes to taking environmental action to prevent further degradation and deterioration of our planet's natural resources. This may require our present generation to assume the costs of the past. Furthermore, if we do not take adequate action we may be further mortgaging the future of our children and grandchildren.

It is clear, however, it will not be possible to bear these environmental costs without some degree of economic and social sacrifice and the challenge is to ensure that its repercussions are kept to the very minimum and that society provides adequate social support for those most severely affected.

Given the potential costs of action to protect the environment and the fact that much of this action will need to be taken by the industrialised countries, how can we ensure that such costs be equitably shared within society? The ILO's tripartite constituents will no doubt wish to have a leading role in seeking solutions to this question.

On the other hand, in view of the severe economic constraints, debt burden and poverty in the Third World, it is likely that the industrialised countries will also need to assist the developing countries significantly in achieving their own development and environment objectives and compensate them for special actions undertaken to improve the global environment. Therefore, a further challenge may be how to convince industrialised countries to help pay some of the environmental costs of developing countries when there are already difficulties in convincing the public in industrialised countries to pay for their own clean-up costs. Again, the international solidarity and tripartite co-operation which have been a major feature of the ILO's work in the past may be called upon to help in planning equitable global action to safeguard the environment in the future.

Public opinion and some governments have drawn particular attention to disarmament and conversion as a potential financial resource to help meet environmental costs. President Gorbachev of the USSR has stated that "We will not be able to save the environment unless we embark on the road of disarmament and release resources for the solution of environmental problems."[1] There is growing interest in the creation of an international fund that would channel some of the resources economised by decreasing military expenditure into global environmental protection and rehabilitation.

TRADITIONAL POLICY OPTIONS AND NEW APPROACHES

Environmental policy has traditionally been based on a regulatory system described as "command and control". It consists of the setting of mandatory environmental standards and their enforcement by government agencies and the legal system. Examples include the setting of emission standards, mandatory use of specific pollution control technologies, product prohibition, and standards or constraints on the use of products. Such policies offer limited flexibility on how to implement the standards and sometimes also entail unequal distribution of the costs of pollution control. *The Economist* has noted that "Regulations [concerning environmental protection] also tend to become a floor as well as a ceiling". No polluter has an incentive to discharge less waste into a local river than the regulations allow; and no entrepreneur has an incentive to devise new technologies that lead to pollution levels below those set by regulations. Furthermore, such regulations have sometimes been made tougher for new entrants to an industry than for the existing firms and this may discourage new investments—even if the new processes are cleaner.[2] Despite such problems, mandatory standards are the most widely used instrument in the environmental protection policy.

Another form of environmental law, however, is based on the "polluter pays principle" and provides for incentive-based regulations. The objective is to ensure that the polluter bears the cost of abating the pollution he causes, while providing more flexibility on how to reach particular emission levels or quality standards, thereby reducing the cost of achieving any given degree of pollution control. Incentive-based regulations include: emission charges for pollutants; fees on products which cause pollution when consumed or discarded; a special licensing fee for a firm or a product: deposit-refund systems, whereby an advance charge is made for "improper disposal" with the potential for a refund.[3]

Pricing policies are another policy instrument which may become increasingly important. As prices of goods and commodities have not traditionally reflected the actual environmental costs of producing them or of extracting and replacing them, or the environmental costs of emissions resulting from their use, such costs have generally had to be borne by society. The development of new pricing policies may be the most direct means of ensuring that the full environmental costs of goods and services are accounted for. This applies particularly when governments own or control resources, such as forest or mineral reserves.[4] Such an approach may have a particular impact on the pricing of commodities (e.g. tropical woods) from developing countries which would be much higher than today if they fully reflected "hidden" costs to the local and global environment.

A further policy instrument which may make a very significant contribution to environmental protection is voluntary action. A large number of enterprises and industrial organisations have established company environmental policies and strategies which have led to substantial investments, management controls, incentives and co-operative efforts with their employees in order to achieve their own environmental objectives—often over and above official emission standards. While such voluntary actions are sometimes criticised because of the lack of monitoring of actual performance concerning non-mandatory standards, they have provided very positive results and may warrant much wider use in the future. Companies which have established such voluntary standards could provide proof of environmental performance which would meet some of the criticism, leading to better collaboration between employers, workers and local communities in achieving cost-efficient ways of meeting common environmental objectives. The time may indeed soon be ripe for a concerted effort to create a collaborative tripartite approach to such issues in future, similar to that achieved for the working environment.

A number of countries are also examining and applying some new policy approaches which may play an increasing role in the future. These include:

The bubble concept and tradeable emission rights: This approach allows firms to modify their own emission levels so long as they maintain an overall level of environmental quality within a given "bubble", or ecosystem. They may trade emission "rights" within the "bubble" with other firms in a given geographical area. This provides industry with an incentive to develop new and better pollution control technology and policies. The bubble system has been applied to air pollution control in the United States and in the Federal Republic of Germany. In future, such systems might include the mandatory reduction of emissions for each transaction so as to improve air quality over time and to ensure that the environment receives more benefits in exchange for the increased flexibility afforded to industry.[5]

Environmental labelling: A number of governments and consumer organisations have established certification of goods that are "environmentally friendly". Such systems provide the information necessary for consumers to make their own judgement concerning the purchase or the additional costs they are willing to pay for a cleaner environment. The certification process, however, is not simple and the setting of appropriate criteria is a complex and often controversial process. Some efforts have also been made to influence government procurement policies so as to support the development of "environmentally friendly" goods and services. Another approach which might have a greater impact on consumers would be to classify some products as "environmentally harmful", which would probably lead to their early demise.[6]

Legal liability: This form of environmental control has been developed in the United States. It places responsibility for environmental damage on the polluters, and the right to demand compensation for environmental damage with the general public provided direct effects are proven. Compensation for pollution can thus be claimed whether or not the companies were acting in compliance with regulations or using mandatory pollution control technology. Such a system of liability would have serious impact on those sectors of industry subject to major industrial accidents and which generate large quantities of toxic and hazardous wastes[7].

International regulations: In recent years a number of regional and international environmental regulations have been adopted in such areas as marine pollution, ozone depleting substances, transboundary air pollution and toxic waste disposal, and nuclear liability. As increasing attention is given to resolving regional and global environmental issues, it may be expected that new international regulations will be developed.

This complex array of environmental policy instruments indicates the wide range of choices available to policy-makers to achieve environmental objectives. Since, moreover, each environmental situation is unique, decisions—whether on the siting of industrial plant, the choice of technologies and processes, the setting of forestry policies, or action to prevent land degradation—must take into account the interplay of many specific factors, including local availability of natural resources, the capacity of the local atmosphere and waters to assimilate emissions, political structures, human resources, social and cultural traditions, the level of economic development and availability of infrastructures, and the potential impact on other areas or countries. As a result, each environmental decision warrants its own set of trade-offs between various technologies, levels of emission, approaches to protection, etc. These decisions may require the active and informed participation of the ILO's constituents, particularly the employers and workers, as well as of a wide range of community groups, women's organisations, non-governmental organisations, etc. Achieving environmentally sound and sustainable development implies popular participation in both developed and developing countries. To ensure that this participation is effective, environmental education and training programmes will be required in order to promote awareness and competence.

ENERGY AND INDUSTRY: CRITICAL FACTORS FOR ENVIRONMENT AND DEVELOPMENT

Since the energy and industrial sectors of national economies are both the source of a significant proportion of pollution and a prerequisite for economic growth and development, environmental policies at all levels may be expected to focus considerable attention on these sectors in the future.

Energy and environment

Accelerated economic and population growth has traditionally been linked to a rise in world energy production and consumption. About three-quarters of the world's energy consumption is in the form of fossil fuels (oil, coal and natural gas), while the remainder is primarily supplied by biomass, hydropower and nuclear power. Projections of energy demand to the year 2000 vary widely, from an optimistic but slight decrease from today's levels to very significant increases.

Developed countries, through conservation of energy for domestic uses and improved efficiency in agriculture and industry, have made significant progress in dissociating economic growth from increases in energy consumption. Nevertheless, in 1985 their share of world energy consumption was more than 75 per cent. In order for the developing countries to meet their industrial, social and economic development objectives, they will require far higher energy consumption.

There are at least four main environmental concerns related to energy which are receiving considerable international attention: the acidification of the atmosphere, mainly due to power stations and car emissions; land degradation due to the unsustainable exploitation of biomass (e.g. fuelwood and charcoal) in developing countries; the potential environmental risk from accidents and the accumulation of radioactive material generated by nuclear power plants; and changes in the world's climate due to the increase in carbon dioxide and other "greenhouse" gases. Much less attention is now being paid to the risk of running out of fossil fuels, as many now are concerned that with global warming the biosphere may cease to be able to absorb the effects of the present pace of energy consumption long before fossil fuels are exhausted.

Energy efficiency is seen by many as a particularly attractive initial policy option for responding to global warming as it leads to a decrease in carbon dioxide emissions, thereby helping to delay global warming, and also makes good economic and environmental sense on its own merits, regardless of the present scientific uncertainty surrounding global climate change.

In the future, therefore, special policies in respect of the energy sector are likely to give fresh impetus to the development and use of new and renewable sources of energy, to energy conservation and to end-use efficiency. New transport and human settlement strategies will aim at minimising society's energy requirements. In addition to their specific effects on workers in the energy sector, such policies will have important repercussions on other energy-using sectors. The ILO's tripartite constituents may wish to play an active role in the policy-making process so as to ensure that these repercussions are as favourable as possible.

Industry and environment

Industry today produces seven times more goods than it did some 40 years ago. It has served as an indispensable engine of growth for modern societies and is essential to developing countries in meeting the growing needs of their people. The Brundtland Report states that "... all nations require and rightly aspire to efficient industrial bases to meet changing needs".[8]

While industrial development has brought obvious benefits, it has also frequently entailed risks of damage to the environment and human health. Despite the significant efforts being made by many enterprises to improve environmental management, the demands that industrial society is placing upon its resource base continue to have profound implications for the environment. Since this overview cannot deal with all environmental issues related to industry, special attention will be given to three issues which have a potentially crucial impact on the environment: chemicals, hazardous waste and industrial accidents.

It is estimated that while there are between 5 and 7 million known chemicals, only about 1,000 of these are produced in substantial quantities. Recent years have seen the number of chemicals increase considerably and the actual quantities produced have risen dramatically as well—for example, from 1 million tons in the 1930s, to 400 million in 1985.

This session of the International Labour Conference will again examine the important question of safety in the use of chemicals at work. The proposed instruments will directly address the improvement of the working and general environment by setting standards for the production, handling, storage, transport, disposal and release of chemicals.

UNEP's International Register of Potentially Toxic Chemicals (IRPTC) and the ILO's safety and health programme work in close collaboration, especially in collecting and compiling information on legal restrictions or the use of chemicals at work. The UNEP/ILO/WHO International Programme on Chemical Safety (IPCS) has produced a set of Environmental Health Criteria documents dealing with chemical and physical pollutants. The IPCS is devising a system of International Chemical Safety Guides and International Chemical Safety Cards to provide special information for the users of chemicals.

The International Occupational Safety and Health Information Centre (CIS) is the ILO's focal point for UNEP's network of national environment-information centres (INFOTERRA) and makes active use of the latter's facilities to disseminate information on chemicals. The CIS further collaborates with over 60 national CIS centres (approximately half of which are in developing countries) with respect to the collection, processing and dissemination of information as a means of improving the working and general environment. The ILO's International Registry of Chemical Safety Information Sheets (IRCIS) contains more than 80,000 of these information sheets in several languages. Each sheet gives detailed advice on chemical hazards and on precautionary measures, including those related to waste removal and disposal.

As a follow-up to the resolution concerning harmonisation of systems of classification and labelling for the use of hazardous chemicals at work, adopted at the 76th Session of the International Labour Conference (1989), the ILO in co-operation with the IPCS has begun to examine, with a view to their harmonisation, the criteria and systems of classification and labelling of chemicals at work which will affect all areas of chemical handling including waste disposal within the working and general environment as well as by private consumers.

The reduction or elimination of hazardous waste together with the monitoring and control of its disposal have become a vital issue. In many countries the related problem of abandoned industrial waste sites has created major pollution problems and, although controls have been introduced by a number of governments, enforcement will be difficult. Developing countries will require special assistance and support—financial and training—in order to cope with the challenge of hazardous waste. Safe disposal requires a co-ordinated effort directed at both the working environment (i.e. the safety and health of workers involved in the disposal activities) and the general environment.

Increasing efforts are being made by industry to develop low- and non-waste technologies that will help to prevent pollution and will allow for the rational use of resources. These technologies include both the in-plant recycling of resources (which lessens the production of waste) and the adaptation of processes to prevent waste. The goal will be not only cleaner production processes, but also cleaner products. As these new technologies are developed, further efforts will be required to promote and facilitate their transfer promptly, economically and equitably.

Industrial disasters have received increasing attention over the past few years, particularly as a result of such major accidents as those at Bhopal, Chernobyl and Schweizerhalle. These accidents are vivid examples of the impact the industrial working environment can have on the general environment, with catastrophic consequences reaching far beyond the waste area. It is important to note that both the scale and the frequency of accidents appears to be increasing. UNEP has reported that the number of major accidents world-wide rose from four (1974-78) to ten (1979-83) and then to 16 (1984-88). Of these 16 accidents, 13 were in developing countries.

Effective response strategies to the growing risk of major industrial accidents call both for preventive measures and emergency preparedness in case more such accidents occur. Following the strong interest expressed by the member States of the European Communities and a number of developing countries, the ILO has already produced a practical manual on the subject and is preparing a code of practice on the prevention of major accident hazards. Technical co-operation projects on major hazard control are already operational in three developing countries with rapidly growing chemical industries. These ILO activities may possibly lead to consideration of international instruments on major hazard control that would be directly relevant to the prevention of serious repercussions on the environment resulting from fires, explosions and the release of toxic substances. Related activities are also being carried out by the OECD, the European Communities, the World Bank and UNIDO. UNEP has launched a new programme called APELL—Awareness and Preparedness for Emergencies at Local Level—which is designed to alert local communities to the potential danger of technological accidents and to provide them with a framework for developing emergency-preparedness plans. The programme would benefit from close collaboration by the social partners.

As industrial technologies have evolved, it has become increasingly clear that when the systems designed to protect plant and workers fail, accidents can ensue whose effects too often spread to the general environment. It is therefore increasingly important for the design, citing, construction and operation of industrial processes to take into account the possible implications for the general environment of failure or breakdown.

NORTH-SOUTH: SEARCHING FOR CONSENSUS

One of the most important issues calling for global co-operation is that of the conflicting perspectives of environmental priorities between North and South. If we are to tackle global environmental problems it is essential to achieve an international consensus on the scope of these problems and to devise efficient policies to deal with their effects; then there must be institutional arrangements to ensure compliance with such policies and the means of financing these global policy responses equitably. Despite the emphasis placed by the Brundtland Report on promoting the rapid development of the Third World as an essential component for the achievement of environmentally sound and sustainable development, increasing concern has been expressed by developing countries that environmental criteria applied by the North may become a new factor of "conditionality" influencing assistance from the developed world and the United Nations system. It is felt that such "conditions" would impose further constraints on development opportunities in the future and even on national sovereignty. Environmental protection measures in the North are also seen by some developing countries as an attempt to protect markets rather than the environment.

Others in developing countries have drawn attention to the fact that while they recognise the importance of environmental protection, the South has been placed in an inequitable situation. Over the years the North has built a strong industrial base, without much regard for the environment during the initial phase, taking advantage of the environment's considerable capacity to absorb and recycle pollution naturally. As a result of pollution generated primarily by the industrialised countries, many scientists believe that the atmosphere is reaching the point when it can no longer absorb additional emissions of certain pollutants without incurring a serious problem of potentially global dimensions. While the North is installing pollution abatement equipment, the South is invited to reject the same "dirty" development strategies used by the North—and to introduce as yet untried "clean" and sustainable technologies developed in the North. This is seen by some critics as detracting from the South's most urgent priority of alleviating widespread poverty and as being likely to promote continued dependence rather than self-reliance. Furthermore, it is sometimes pointed out that the real issue is not "clean" technology but the fact that the developed countries are using up a disproportionate share of global resources such as energy and raw materials.

In the light of statements made at recent international conferences and meetings, it might be said that generally the developed countries are giving very high priority to strategies that will solve the environmental problems resulting from their prosperity and past industrialisation, whereas the developing countries must give first priority to strategies to solve their immediate basic development and poverty problems, while also meeting their own environmental objectives.

It is interesting to note that many of the concerns, doubts and signs of mistrust and frustration attributable to the North-South debate are also becoming increasingly evident as regards local environmental problems and policies within nations, between rural and urban areas and between poor and wealthy segments of society.

EAST-WEST: ADAPTING TO RAPID CHANGE

As this Report is being written in late 1989, the world is observing a very rapid change in Eastern Europe which will have a lasting influence not only on Europe but on the world political and economic scene. These changes will also have important implications for the environment.

Following many decades of what has now been admitted by various official sources in Poland, Hungary and the USSR as a neglect of the environment, the opportunity exists for a new and collaborative relationship between individual European nations and within regional and international organisations to foster a major effort to assist the countries of Eastern Europe in their environmental, economic, political and social reforms.

Many bilateral East-West activities are being considered which may lead to direct assistance in environmental protection and rehabilitation. They will entail providing important resources in the form of economic credits, grants, technology transfers, policy advice, technical assistance and specialised training programmes.

In many countries concern for environment issues has provided a focus for participation by the public and by independent organisations in governmental decisions, this concern subsequently extending to wider issues of democratic reform and freedoms. Environmental co-operation has already shown itself to be a good example of the concept of "confidence building measures" developed at the Helsinki Conference on Security and Co-operation in Europe.

I see an opportunity for the Office to support the ILO's constituents, especially the employers and workers, in playing a more active role in promoting collaboration in Europe on environmental protection and rehabilitation in such areas as employment and structural adjustment, training, working environment and technology transfer.

ENVIRONMENT AND TRADE POLICIES: COMPETITION OR CO-OPERATION

Some countries are concerned that environmental policies may lead to a new form of trade protection or unfair trading practices.

The prospect of trade constraints being imposed for environmental reasons is causing particular concern among developed countries. The number of environmental criteria and standards are growing rapidly in industrialised countries—and groupings of industrialised countries, such as the European Community. Governments and industry have become increasingly anxious lest such criteria and standards impose significant costs and constraints on production processes or specific products, thereby undermining their competitive advantage unless their trading partners adopt similar standards and criteria. But issues of unfair competitive advantage due to lower environmental standards are not the only international trade issues. Criticism has also arisen about specific regulations which are so restrictive in what are deemed to be unnecessary details as to constitute an environmental "non-tariff" barrier to the import of otherwise harmless goods. On the other hand, some countries have stated adamantly that they have the sovereign right and responsibility to establish environmental standards as they see appropriate, and what appear to an exporting country as restrictive environmental criteria may be seen in the importing country as important environmental safeguards.

Other issues related to environmental policies and trade include the international transport and export of hazardous waste and of substances banned in the exporting country, particularly to countries without adequate waste disposal facilities; the export of such substances without prior informed consent being obtained; the export of hazardous machinery or technological processes; and simply the transfer of polluting industries to other countries so as to avoid the costs of meeting strict national environmental standards.

From the perspective of the International Labour Organisation, all these relatively new and unexplored environmental and trade issues may have important implications for the world of work, particularly as regards employment, economic growth, occupational safety and health, the prevention of industrial accidents and industrial relations. While in the past the ILO has not been actively involved in the preliminary discussions concerning these issues, e.g. within GATT, UNEP and various regional economic organisations, it may be useful for the Office to monitor future discussions with a view to ensuring that such implications are taken into account in the preparation of new trade agreements and of arrangements linked to the environment.

Notes

[1] Cited by Mr. E. Shevardnadze in "Ecology and diplomacy", Press Bulletin No. 223, Permanent Mission of the Soviet Union (Geneva, 29 Nov. 1989).

[2] "The politics of posterity", by Frances Cairncross in *The Economist* (special environment survey issue entitled "Costing the earth") (London, 2 Sep. 1989), p. 9.

[3] UBS, Phillips and Drew: *Investing in a green Europe* (London, Oct. 1989), p. 8.

[4] W. D. Ruckelshaus: "Towards a sustainable world", in *Scientific American* (special issue entitled "Managing planet earth"), Vol. 261, No. 3, Sep. 1989), p. 118.

[5] *Investing in a green Europe*, op. cit., pp. 8-9.

[6] ibid., p. 9.

[7] loc. cit.

[8] *Our common future*, report of the World Commission on Environment and Development (Oxford, OUP, 1987), p. 206.

POTENTIAL REPERCUSSIONS ON THE WORLD OF WORK

3

While there is now a considerable amount of scientific information on environmental issues and growing documentation on environmental policies, comparatively little research on analysis is available on the repercussions of environmental problems and policies on the world of work. For example, despite the great interest shown in the inter-relationship between environment and employment over the past decade, particularly in the industrialised countries, there remains a lack of precision in the scope and underlying assumptions of much of the research to date. Environment is still an area in which statistics are often irregular, scattered and non-comparable. One of the causes is the lack of a uniform definition of the term "environment" itself: some definitions include almost all activities related to natural resources and ecology, while others are limited to action taken to prevent pollution or to rehabilitate areas already damaged by pollution. A similar confusion exists in many studies concerning the scope of the term "employment": some restrict it to direct employment created as a result of pollution-control activities, while others use sophisticated input-output models to estimate the indirect and long-term employment effects of environmental policies, including their general economic implications.

Similar problems of precision arise when one tries to examine the boundaries and linkages between the working and general environment. For example, emissions from one industry may directly affect the working environment of workers in another industry, as when air pollution from a factory affects construction workers or agricultural workers outside.

It is thus difficult to isolate repercussions on the world of work, much more measure them in quantitative terms. This is particularly so when one looks at the special environmental problems linked to poverty in rural and urban areas of developing countries. Such analytical constraints, however, should not prevent us from focusing attention on these issues with a view to identifying the repercussions which either occur already or which might develop in the future.

THE ENVIRONMENT IN RELATION TO EMPLOYMENT, POVERTY AND DEVELOPMENT

Environment and employment

As noted above, the analysis of linkages between environmental policies and employment is severely constrained by the lack of comparable and valid data in industrialised countries and the situation is even worse in developing countries. Nevertheless, a number of national reports and studies have been carried out which provide some insights into possible effects on employment, particularly in industrial activities.

For example, evidence in industrialised market-economy countries suggests that adverse employment effects of plant closures attributable to environmental policy have been very limited. Plants that allegedly closed for environmental reasons were mostly small, old and marginal, and probably would have closed anyway. In many instances, environmental regulations simply accelerated the timing.[1] According to a United States report, between 1971 and 1983 the closure of 155 plants as a result of pollution-control regulations resulted in the loss of only 32,899 jobs.[2]

Plant closures, however, are only part of the environment/employment story. The adverse effects on employment may have been greater in cases where plants did not expand or could not be built at all because of environmental regulations. Unfortunately, almost no data are available to measure such effects in the past, nor to help predict potential repercussions in the future.

Taking into account the need for a massive global effort concerning environmental protection and rehabilitation, however, one can foresee both very considerable opportunities for job creation and areas of potentially significant job losses. For example, in the European Communities, where the level of technology is high, improved environmental protection may have a favourable effect on employment thanks to the manufacture, installation and maintenance of pollution abatement equipment, the development and implementation of new environmentally-sound tecnologies and the increased need for specialised environmental management staff. In Eastern Europe, on the other hand, urgently-needed environmental protection measures may lead to the closure of obsolete and uneconomical plants, resulting in significant job losses. Some of these losses may, however, be offset by major, though more short-term, employment opportunities arising out of large-scale environmental rehabilitation projects.

For example, in Poland, in the region of Gdansk and, to a lesser extent, Silesia, plant closures in application of environmental regulations have been significant and have aggravated unemployment problems. In the Soviet Union the economic and environmental consequences of the large irrigation system that has drained the Aral Sea have likewise proved negative. The resulting increase in the salinity of agricultural land has devastated the local economy, eliminated a large number of jobs and forced part of the local population to move to other regions.

Macroeconomic studies in many OECD countries have evaluated the direct and indirect employment effects of specific environmental programmes. The studies suggest that the overall net effect of environmental policies on employment were very small and that although

it was positive in the short term, these positive effects diminished over time as they were outweighed by the increased costs and prices of the products of the polluting industries.[3] Research supported by the European Communities also indicates that the effects of environmental policies on employment levels have usually been small and insignificant relative to the influence of other variables in the labour market and that while in the short run the direct employment effects have usually been positive, a few studies suggest that once the indirect effects have also been taken into account, the overall employment effect may have been neutral or slightly negative.

A study prepared for the European Communities states that although almost every conceivable claim has been made concerning the relationship between environmental protection and economic development (including employment creation), such claims may be grouped around one or other of two contrasting viewpoints:

(a) a strict environmental policy can have an inflationary effect, retard economic growth, reduce productive investment, lead to business closures and result in losses of jobs; and

(b) a more effective environmental policy can stimulate technological progress and more cost-effective methods of pollution control and resource use, encourage new forms of enterprise and stimulate economic development and growth of job opportunities.[4]

As the study goes on to emphasise, however, a careful examination of the underlying relationship involved indicates that it is not possible to support either of these viewpoints as a generally valid statement. It appears that the relationship between employment and environment is an empirical (rather than theoretical) matter whether in a given situation the relationship has been beneficial or harmful. It is therefore extremely difficult to draw valid conclusions or to formulate generalisations about the relationship between environmental policies and employment.

Most of the research and analysis carried out has focused on the employment effects of environmental policies in industry. Nevertheless, even in the industrialised countries, environmental policies

related to agriculture, transport, tourism, fisheries, forests, wildlife, etc., may also have very important employment and income implications. Regrettably, even less information exists on these sectors and further efforts to examine employment/environment linkages are needed.

Another factor often overlooked is that of job maintenance, which can be achieved by protecting environmental resources. Examples are the limitations on drift-net fishing to prevent the depletion of fish stocks; the protection of employment in mining though the use of new technologies permitting the leaching of minerals from low grade deposits and mine tailings; and the protection of employment in forestry by preventing forest damage resulting from air pollution, particularly acid rain. Conversely, environmental accidents such as oil and chemical "spills" have had adverse effects on employment. In order to be able to protect employment and incomes effectively in such situations policy-makers need an advance warning system so that they can respond early enough and with appropriate resources. Employers and workers could be an important source of information for such early warning systems, as well as promoters of appropriate environmental action. One of the criteria to be included in any assessment of environmental policies and projects, therefore, is their effect on employment and incomes—not only in a given enterprise but in entire communities.

Another aspect often ignored concerns the differences between locally and nationally aggregated effects of environmental policies on employment: in other words, while the loss or gain of jobs attributed to environment may be relatively minor nationally, their effects in a local community can be very disruptive. From the ILO's perspective, therefore, special priority should be given to those workers who may lose their jobs or who may require training and adjustment assistance in order to take up new employment opportunities related to new environmental activities or other alternative employment.

As a first step to expanding its understanding of these issues, the ILO convened a Tripartite Meeting of Experts on Employment and

Training Implications of Environmental Policies in Europe (Geneva, 20 Nov.-5 Dec. 1989). A report was prepared for the meeting which examined the employment effects of environmental programmes, the job-creation effects of employment programmes that have a significant environmental component, and also the skill and training implications of pursuing environmental policies in Europe.[5] The meeting held a very lively and frank exchange of views concerning these issues and adopted a number of conclusions which will provide useful guidance for future action by the ILO's constituents and the Office.[6]

There are several new issues related to environment and employment which deserve special consideration. The very high priority being given by the international community to the global issues of climate change and ozone depletion may result in policy responses which could have significant and yet, to date, unforeseen employment and social implications.

While considerable scientific and diplomatic progress has been made concerning the control of substances that deplete the ozone layer, particularly chloroflurocarbons (CFCs), there has been little progress in our understanding of the potential economic and social implications of new control policies—and specifically the employment and income effects (i) in the companies which produce or use CFCs; (ii) in companies producing alternatives to CFCs; (iii) in companies which provide technical services and equipment to adapt the equipment of present CFC users to the new alternatives; and, finally, (iv) in the general economy due to the significant investments required and the additional environmental costs involved. Quantitatively, we have very limited information concerning the actual numbers of jobs which may be created or lost.

This lack of information concerning the possible economic, employment and social effects of technological innovation needs to be remedied—and not simply for academic reasons. The information is necessary for policy decisions if we are to achieve the most cost-effective responses to new environmental challenges. Very tentative estimates have been made concerning the economic costs of measures to replace CFCs. To produce substitutes for CFCs may require an investment programme of approximately US$6 billion over the next ten years. In addition, the replacement cost of existing equipment using CFCs could cost as much as US$150 billion over the next 25 years (most of that, of course, would be normal replacement costs). This equipment includes very large refrigeration systems for food preservation, transportation and processing, as well as air conditioning systems for large buildings. There would also be an effect on consumers; for example, approximately US$20 to 30 billion worth of domestic freezers and refrigerators dependent on CFCs are used in Western Europe alone. Any regulations to phase this equipment out more rapidly will greatly increase the costs of such environmental policies.[7]

The manner and timing of the replacement of CFCs will be an important factor influencing social and economic effects. An immediate ban could have disruptive effects, even if it were feasible to convert all the equipment now using CFCs in a very brief time-span. In addition, new and unforeseen hazards related to the use of substitutes may be encountered. Therefore, the views of the employers and workers need to be taken into account in designing environmental policies. Furthermore, developing countries which have recently invested in CFC production facilities or CFC-dependent equipment could incur significant economic losses for which they might not be fully compensated despite the provisions on special assistance in the Montreal Protocol on Substances that Deplete the Ozone Layer.

Scientific knowledge is changing so rapidly that chemical manufacturers may be concerned that in a few years' time the big investments required to develop and produce CFC alternatives may become unproductive because of new and more appropriate alternatives surpassing the first generation of substitutes. This environmentally-related uncertainty could have a delaying effect on investment decisions and on the development of innovative products—as well as lead to economic losses.

The potential employment and income implications of some of the present policy discussions or scenarios to deal with global warming, such as taxes on CO_2 emissions or large-scale reductions in emissions of CO_2 and other "greenhouse" gases over various target periods, are even more difficult to assess. In almost all cases they will have an important impact on the energy, transport and industrial sectors of our economies. Should we not carefully assess the potential implications of various policy responses so as to ensure that the employment and income effects are indeed taken into account at the earliest possible stage? These issues are so vital that the ILO's tripartite constituents need to be involved more actively in the policy-making process.

This discussion of environment and employment, however, raises several fundamental questions concerning the future. Are the shocks to our economies and labour market created by structural adjustment driven by pressures of finance and debt any different from the shocks which might be created by new environmental policies? Will the environmental pressures for structural and technological change be relatively small—or more substantial than now anticipated? Are the policy responses which have been developed to support and facilitate present-day structural adjustment also applicable to potential new environmental adjustments? Are the kinds of innovative efforts needed to ensure that the labour market is sufficiently flexible, mobile and skilled to be able to shift from one area to another to facilitate structural adjustment policies the same as those required to help industry and other sectors of the economy to adapt to more environmentally sound and sustainable practices?

In other words, is the environment just another factor to be integrated within the overall effort to achieve structural adjustment and technological change—or is it sufficiently unique and significant that it should be treated separately? Given the potential additional capital costs involved in environmental protection, will the latter constrain the on-going process of structural adjustment? An additional issue which may suggest that environment may need to be treated separately is the fact that the national priorities of developing countries vis-à-vis environment may indeed be quite different from those perceived by some industrialised countries as global priorities. This disparity in perception of priority may become an important factor in future international and regional discussions on environment and development.

Environment and poverty and development

While the issues related to employment discussed above are primarily focused on highly industrialised sectors of the economy, the majority of the world's population is confronted by different environmental challenges dominated by the complex relationship between environment and poverty and development. In developing countries, the environment plays a very significant role in the daily lives and work of both the rural and urban populations.

The Brundtland Report firmly expresses the view that poverty "is a major cause and effect of global environmental problems". It states that "a world in which poverty is endemic will always be prone to ecological and other catastrophes". It stresses that the satisfaction of basic needs in the developing countries is essential to achieving sustainable development and emphasises that "The most basic of all needs is for a livelihood: that is, employment". Recognising the non-sustainable pressures placed on the land and water resources in many rural areas of developing countries, in order to support the rapidly growing population, the report describes the crucial need for more non-agricultural employment opportunities in rural areas as essential to limiting the uncontrolled growth of urban areas. It further points out that in most developing countries "between one-fourth and one-half of the economically active urban population cannot find adequate, stable livelihoods", although many poor people "are in fact working 10 to 15 hours a day, six to seven days a week". It concludes that "their problem is not so much underemployment as underpayment."[8]

It is poverty which is responsible for the destruction of ecological resources—not the poor and landless people who have no alternative but to violate ecological imperatives in order to survive.

Given the dependence of the rural poor on agriculture, land degradation and inadequate fresh water supplies have in many areas led to increased poverty and made it impossible for them to survive on the land, particularly the subsistence farmers, women and tribal populations. Such environmental constraints exist not only in the well-known drought and desertification areas like the Sahel, but also in many other ecosystems such as rainforests, and mountain and coastal areas. Similarly, the urban poor are confronted with severe problems related to housing conditions, the availability of fuel, water and sanitation facilities as well as transport.

The pressures of rural and urban poverty have a direct effect on levels of employment and income rarely revealed in traditional economic and employment statistics. They most certainly exist, however, and require the attention of governments, employers and workers and of the international community.

The linkage between poverty alleviation and employment, for instance, is dramatically and concretely demonstrated by the application of genetic engineering to crops for increasing herbicide resistance. On the one hand, this development encourages the excessive use of chemical herbicides by farmers, thereby degrading the environment in industrialised and developing countries alike. On the other hand, it will not only introduce a new fixed cost to the poor farmers of the Third World by forcing them to purchase the herbicide genetically tied to the seed, but will also strike a colossal blow at the poor. In the developing countries, particularly in Asia, manual weeding provides a major source of farm employment and cash income for hired labour, including women from the poorest households who will no longer be required.[9]

A critical issue for the ILO in future will be to help define new policies to alleviate poverty which will also achieve environmental and employment and income objectives.

Is it necessary for developing countries to follow the same development strategy as that followed by the developed countries which, while achieving high levels of growth, gave relatively low priority to environmental protection? It has been seen that most developed countries followed a strategy of resource-intensive (energy and materials) growth which led to significant deterioration of the environment. Later, as perceptions changed, incomes grew and shifts were made to less resource-intensive economic growth, there was an improvement in environmental quality through a combination of corrective and preventive efforts, including new technologies and changes in products and processes. In other words, the trade-offs between growth and environmental quality change over time, particularly as incomes and consumption rise.

Despite the suggestions in some circles that developing countries must go through similar stages of development (i.e. economic growth with environmental degradation, slowly followed by improvements resulting from environmental efforts), this need not and should not be so. Developing countries are taking and will continue to take advantage of the many technological advances to prevent or mitigate environmental degradation and therefore should not have to repeat the "unsustainable" patterns of the past.

In order to achieve global environmental objectives, however, all countries will need to adopt the most up-to-date industrial processes and technologies incorporating environmental improvements. Nevertheless, as new "clean" processes and special environmental protection technologies may indeed be more expensive than traditional ones, new approaches and mechanisms (including financial incentives) to facilitate rapid and global dissemination of these new technologies will be required. It is expected, therefore, that issues related to the transfer of environmental technologies will receive considerable attention at the United Nations Conference on Environment and Development in 1992 as well as during the preparation of the International Development Strategy for the Fourth United Nations Development Decade.

The Office, too, is concerned by the implications of such development patterns. The apparent linkage between economic growth and environmental deterioration needs to be severed, just as many countries over the past 15 years have so dramatically severed similar linkages between energy comsumption and gross national product. The change in the energy/GNP relationship has occurred mainly as a result of the unnerving fluctuations of and drastic increases in energy prices. Is there any prospect of the same sort of change coming about in environmental terms?

Can the developing countries absorb an "environmental shock" to their economies in the 1990s like the "energy shock" of the 1970s? If changes are required, how can they be achieved more gradually so as to avoid upheavals like those experienced in the energy sector which led to disruption and stagnation in many economies? Furthermore, given the high level of debt and poverty in many developing countries today, can such countries be expected to finance the additional costs of the environmental quality standards needed to meet global challenges such as ozone depletion and global warming? And, a question of particular concern to the ILO, if developing countries must pay a significant share of those additional costs, will it be at the expense of their employment and social objectives, including urgent action to alleviate poverty?

Another relevant development policy issue is whether developing countries which are expanding their exports of natural resources such as timber and fish and cash crops grown on previously forested land areas, should be expected to give up those exports for environmental reasons. Can deeply-indebted countries accept additional financial pressures or further reduce imports to compensate for decreasing their exports? How can countries in such a situation be adequately compensated for environmental action that leads to economic disruption? What measures will be required to ensure that the particular workers and people affected by such action actually receive the benefits of the compensation? What kind of new development strategy would be necessary to achieve significant and sustainable develop- ment without environmental degradation?

These are all questions which will require careful consideration and discussion during the 1990s and probably beyond. For its part, the Office is actively participating in the preparations being undertaken throughout the United Nations system for a new International Development Strategy for the Fourth United Nations Development Decade currently under discussion and negotiation. The new strategy is expected to include environmental considerations as well as employment and income generation as important objectives.

In addition to these broad policy issues, however, there are a number of specific issues related to poverty and development which are of particular concern to the ILO and should also be mentioned.

Women

In many developing countries women are the first to suffer from the degradation of the environment in carrying out their traditional tasks of fetching water and fuel, food production and cooking and other family responsibilities. In all these areas, the degradation of land, forest and water resources have a direct impact on their daily lives, work, health and even survival.

Because of their knowledge and experience of the possibilities and limitations of local natural and living resources, women, particularly in developing countries, are also the first line of defence and protection of the environment. They are in fact the key managers of natural resources in many developing countries.[10] Unfortunately, too often their experience and knowledge are ignored in the development process in both rural and urban areas, to the detriment of the environment. Effective measures need to be taken to ensure that women are able to play a more active role in the design, development, selection and implementation of development policies and projects, particularly those related to the natural and agricultural resources necessary for their livelihood and survival.

For example, only recently has attention been given to the health implications of the use of biomass fuels by women for cooking and heating—often the cause of serious respiratory and eye problems—as a result of very high levels of indoor pollution.[11] Furthermore, women as the principal agricultural workforce in many parts of the world are often exposed, without proper training or warning, to agricultural chemicals both in their work in the fields and through the water and foods they collect and use in their daily lives.

It is important that account be taken of these matters in all development programmes and policies; the ILO's constituents could play a more active role in this regard at the national and international levels.

Indigenous and tribal peoples

At the last session of the Conference the Indigenous and Tribal Peoples Convention, 1989, was adopted. As noted in the section above concerning environment and development issues, these peoples are often the victims of degradation of the environment. This has been particularly stressed in the media in respect of the indigenous forest peoples in the Amazonian and other tropical rain forests. Less attention has been given to other tribal peoples living in vulnerable ecological areas, e.g. desert nomads (such as the Tuareg, Bedouin and San), the Arctic tribes (Innuit, Sami) and others in the mountain, coastal and temperate areas of the world.

Action to protect ecologically vulnerable areas will at the same time protect the livelihood and culture of indigenous peoples. But this is only part of the picture, because the world has also much to learn from the experience of these peoples in environmental management, which they have been practising for centuries. Their cultures, economies and ethics are focused on practical approaches to sustainable development which have enabled them to live in harmony with their natural environment. The international community has an interest in learning from their experience, knowledge of and respect for the natural environment to help us to achieve practical models and approaches to sustainable development on a global scale.

Labour-intensive infrastructure

The ILO's programme of labour-intensive infrastructure development, for example, is actively involved in a wide range of environmental improvement activities such as afforestation, irrigation, flood protection and land rehabilitation. Such labour-intensive approaches to environmental protection and rehabilitation are particularly appropriate as they emphasise active local and community participation which helps to ensure that local priorities are met and the public works effectively managed and maintained. Such programmes benefit both rural and urban populations and help to achieve both environmental and employment objectives. In addition, such activities could make an important contribution to achieving the objectives of the United Nations International Decade for Natural Disaster Reduction. The ILO's tripartite constituents can play a vital role in ensuring the development and expansion of such projects in developing countries.

Agriculture and food security

The Brundtland Report devoted special attention to the challenge of agriculture and food security and their critical relationship to the environment. The raising of global food production will be constrained by the growing crisis of land degradation referred to above. At the same time, as a result of efforts to shift to more intensive agricultural activities on increasingly marginal lands, land degradation will be accelerated, placing the planet on a dangerous path towards escalating food security problems.

However, global food security is not simply a question of total food production; it also implies that all people, even the poorest, are able to get food. While distortions in the world food market must be reduced, much can be achieved by national governments dealing with such critical factors as the inequitable distribution of productive assets (particularly land and water resources), inappropriate policies (e.g. excessive subsidies for irrigation, fertilisers, and pesticides which often lead to environmental damage to land and water resources), traditional neglect of the small producers, and insufficient infrastructural facilities.

The Brundtland Report emphasised that rapid, sound agricultural development would mean both more food and more opportunities for people to earn money to buy food. It noted that shifting production to food-deficient countries and to the resource-poor farmers within those countries could provide secure and sustainable livelihoods. This may contribute to conserving land and water resources, slow rural-to-urban migration and, by combating poverty, help to slow population growth. Nevertheless, the obstacles to achieving such shifts in production should not be underestimated. To achieve these goals will require a major effort to provide the rural poor—including, especially, rural women—with improved access to productive assets, including land, credit, technology, skills, infrastructure, etc. Some of the proposals and suggestions arising from the 1988 Conference discussion on rural employment promotion and the present session's discussion on self-employment may provide some useful insights for the ILO and others on how to improve action in this sea.

Urban poor

The poor in urban areas who are deprived of access to adequate housing, water and sewage facilities are caught up in a "vicious circle" of poverty and environmental deterioration. A dynamic policy to respond to the basic infrastructure needs of the urban poor could convert that circle into a "virtuous" one, providing access to employment and income opportunities as well as simultaneously improving the urban working and living environment. The very high levels of urban air pollution in many developing countries may be a matter of mutual interest and potential collaboration between the developed and developing countries. A major programme to deal with the problem would imply drastic and costly decisions, which most governments have had to postpone because of lack of funds and sometimes the political resistance of concerned groups. Are there opportunities for new urban assistance programmes to assist industry, small and medium enterprises, the transport sector—public and private—and households to achieve significantly lower air pollution levels? Could such measures lead to new employment opportunities? How might national and local employers' and workers' organisations collaborate in such programmes?

All these issues—and, of course, there are also many others which could be mentioned—indicate areas in which there are opportunities for the ILO's tripartite constituents and the ILO itself to respond to the special environmental challenges of the urban and rural poor of developing countries. In fact, the most important contribution the ILO could make to environmentally sound and sustainable development may be to reinforce its on-going activities related to poverty alleviation and support to local, popular participation and to identifying new and innovative ways to help the rural and urban poor to meet their own special development and environmental objectives.

TRAINING AND THE ENVIRONMENT

Training is an essential factor in environment-related employment creation. Skilled manpower is required for the employment opportunities created through the design, manufacture, installation and maintenance of environmental equipment, as well as for environmental management and administration at the government and enterprise levels, and to meet environmental education and training needs.

While considerable attention and resources are now being directed to meeting such training needs through international technical co-operation and government-assisted training programmes, matched by significant efforts by industry, these specialist skills are, in fact, only the very tip of the environmental training iceberg. In order to achieve environmentally sound and sustainable development, environmental considerations should be fully integrated into all education and training activities. This applies equally to the ILO's special areas of concern, i.e. vocational, management and occupational safety and health training, as well as training for artisans, co-operative workers and women, and general education.

A new "environmental ethic"—new attitudes and approaches to environmental protection—is needed if the 6 billion people sharing this planet in the year 2000 are to enjoy an improved quality of work and life.

Part of the major effort required to transfer environmental technologies from the industrially advanced countries of the West to developing countries and to Eastern Europe will be the transfer of skills and training. Given the high costs of environmental equipment and related "clean" technological processes, sufficient resources for training must be included in initial project design and financing arrangements. Governments will need to devote particular attention to upgrading the environmental knowledge and awareness of their staff in the various technical, information, administration and legal services.

Governments in developing countries will need to give priority to training staff for specific environmental activities, such as the preparation of environmental assessments, planning strategies and policies; environmental monitoring and impact assessments; and the design and development of appropriate data bases. In order for the developing countries to play their full role in international environmental agreements, conventions and their application, a special international effort will be required to support the human resources development needs in governments, industry and research institutions. Agreements to deal with global environmental issues cannot be effective unless the political, economic, social and cultural views of all countries are effectively represented in the policy-making process. Special programmes to support the participation of developing countries within the Inter-Governmental Panel on Climate Change have been instituted. Given the ILO's experience in manpower planning and training needs assessment, the Office could provide assistance in identifying skill gaps in developing countries, taking account of future environmental priorities; it could also extend assistance to training institutions to help them meet identified needs in the most practical, co-ordinated and timely manner.

Employers will be particularly affected by the changing skill requirements related to environmental management within enterprises and the application of new environmental technologies, processes and procedures. Much of this expertise required by enterprises can be provided through on-the-job training of managers and technical personnel in up-to-date environmental management techniques. Environmental objectives can provide new and attractive incentives and opportunities and even create new enterprises, including small and medium-sized ones. In such cases, they will need to be able to find skilled manpower in the local labour market to meet their requirements, otherwise manpower could become an important constraint to the development of such new enterprises.

THE WORKING ENVIRONMENT AND THE GENERAL ENVIRONMENT: TWO SIDES OF THE SAME COIN

The working environment, which received relatively little emphasis in the Brundtland Report and UNEP's *Environmental perspective,* has a very high priority in the ILO, which has a constitutional mandate to assist countries in improving their working environment. Since 1919 it has been pursuing this aim, especially through its Conventions and Recommendations, Codes of Practice, research, publications, technical co-operation, tripartite meetings and advisory services.

It is beyond the terms of this Report to provide a detailed review of the extensive action taken or planned by the ILO and by governments and employers' and workers' organisations in this field. Rather, the goal is to draw attention to the growing interaction between the working and general environment and to several specific issues which demonstrate how the traditional distinction between them has become blurred. This change provides new opportunities for integrated action to improve both the working and the general environment.

Many problems in the general environment have their causes in the working environment. Many of the pollutants and hazards originally identified as occupational hazards have an effect far beyond the workplace. The rising number of major industrial accidents and their impact on entire communities and even globally provide dramatic evidence that what happens within the plant deeply affects the safety, health and welfare of the local population and the general environment. It is not only industrial accidents that show the interaction between the working environment and the general environment, for the link exists in the day-to-day activities of most sectors of the economy—industry, transport, agriculture, mining, energy, etc.

As noted in the 1987 General Survey *Safety in the working environment* by the Committee of Experts on the Application of Conventions and Recommendations, "It is ... in the working environment that the primary control should be exercised, and the approach taken should be that of ensuring co-ordination between the general environment and the working environment."[12] The first ILO instrument to draw attention to this inter-relationship was the Working Environment (Air Pollution, Noise and Vibration) Recommendation, 1977 (No. 156), Paragraph 15 of which states: "In prescribing measures for the prevention and control of air pollution, noise and vibration in the working environment, the competent authority should take account of the relationship between the protection of the working environment and the protection of the general environment."

In a report to the United Nations General Assembly, the Governing Body stated: "Lasting solutions to the problems of the working environment can be found only in the broader context of the improvement of the general environment. Similarly, the problems of the general environment cannot be satisfactorily tackled unless the problems of the working environment are effectively solved."[13]

The ILO is consequently intensifying its efforts to integrate problems of the general environment within its activities for the working environment. It will be equally important for the ILO's tripartite constituents to work towards a more integrated approach to the working and general environment in their national and enterprise-level activities, not only from a technical point of view, but also from the administrative and institutional angles.

Looking to the future, a number of issues call for increased attention:

— Well managed safety and health programmes at the workplace will make an important contribution to the protection of the general environment.

— Adverse repercussions for the working environment may result from the technologies used to control pollution emissions from enterprises or related to the rehabilitation of land (e.g. cleaning up waste-disposal sites). More research and closer tripartite collaboration may help to identify such potential repercussions at an early stage, so that they may be prevented or remedied.

— This session of the Conference will be completing its second discussion on safety in the use of chemicals at work. In this context, due attention should be given to the need to protect the general environment when formulating standards on the working environment.

— Since workers have mostly been the first to be exposed to chemicals and hazardous substances within the workplace, their organisations are very actively involved in efforts to prevent such hazards. Their experience and views in this regard may be helpful in the design of policy responses to these same issues within the general environment. Proven mechanisms, such as joint health and safety committees, might therefore be expanded so as to include general environmental issues. Furthermore, consideration should be given to the possibility of using existing labour and factory inspection mechanisms, including occupational safety and health institutes, to help with environmental monitoring and inspection at the plant level. This might also promote more effectively integrated action within the enterprise, as well as the rationalisation of inspection machinery, which is often confronted with serious financial and human resource constraints, especially in developing countries. As noted in the *Nordic Programme for the Environment*, environmental control and supervision "should take place as near to production as possible, in collaboration with the work environment authorities".[14]

The ILO's constitutional obligation to help to achieve adequate protection for the life and health of workers in every occupation becomes all the more awesome when one bears in mind that there is a working environment for every task performed on this planet. Furthermore, in view of the rapid increase in the world's population, millions of new jobs will need to be created and the Organisation's challenge will be to help to ensure that these jobs are safe, environmentally sound and sustainable.

So far the Office—like many national governments—has given top priority to the working environment of industrial and other organised sectors of the economy. Efforts to increase the priority accorded to that of the other sectors, including the informal sector, will need to be reinforced. Special efforts may also be required in respect of such categories of workers as indigenous and tribal peoples; the landless poor and subsistence farmers; unorganised agricultural and plantation workers; workers in the informal urban sector; and workers in small enterprises.

Workers in the informal sector, for example, are often exposed to very hazardous working environments through the generally high levels of urban air and water pollution, the use of various noxious material and fuels and the fact that they often work in open or unprotected areas. A further example is the gold mining sector in Latin America and Asia where exposure to mercury during the separation processes used by many "informal" and independent gold mining operations has created serious problems for the workers involved as well as for others who use the waters which have been polluted by mercury.

Action to improve the working environment for these particularly vulnerable groups within our societies would also have a positive impact on the general environment. In fact, in many of these examples the working environment cannot be distinguished from the general environment.

While considerable attention has been given to exposure to specific chemicals within industrial enterprises, less has been given to the potential dangers of day-to-day cumulative exposure or even combined exposure to chemicals and substances. In other words, a relatively specialised approach has been followed in which the potential effects of individual chemicals are analysed and specific conclusions drawn regarding possible threshold levels of exposure. While such action is indeed necessary, and much more information is required about many old and new chemicals, it may not provide a sufficiently integrated approach to the overall impact of exposure to chemicals upon the life of workers and their families and communities. For example, many workers are exposed to more than one chemical during their working life and we are not fully aware of the combined or cumulative effects. Furthermore, do we know all we should about the possible interaction of the exposure at the workplace with that in the general environment—as in the case of urban air and water pollution and radiation?

Given the rising fears of workers which have led to efforts by some to promote a "zero exposure" approach, the tripartite partners need to collaborate more closely in identifying the most effective and efficient policies for dealing with such complex issues. As the cost of achieving close to "zero exposure" levels can be several levels of magnitude higher than that of achieving even 95 per cent or higher control levels, an integrated approach would be required in order to make effective use of available financial and scientific resources to achieve the optimal protection of workers and the general environment. In the past this has been seen as a scientific exercise but in fact the management of risk reduction is a political, economic and social exercise requiring the informed collaboration of governments, employers, workers and society. Ministries of labour can ensure that conditions in the working environment are properly monitored and verified as to the most appropriate threshold levels; employers have an important role in providing information and carrying out research into the toxic effects of chemicals that are being used or developed; and workers need to ensure that effective protection is provided both for themselves and for the general population.

Current efforts in many countries to implement practical and economically feasible solutions to the most important and urgent working environment issues need to be strengthened and further extended to various working populations not yet receiving adequate protection. Training and information activities will play a particularly important role in the improvement of the working and general environment. The ILO's International Programme for the Improvement of Working Conditions and Environment (PIACT) could play a key role in developing a new global response to these critical issues bound up with the ILO's mandate.

ENVIRONMENT AND INDUSTRIAL RELATIONS

The growing priority given by workers' and employers' organisations to protecting and improving the environment is a logical extension of their long-standing concern for the conditions of work and life of the working populations. What is new, however, is the growing recognition by both employers and workers that their common concerns (e.g. working environment, employment, training, economic growth of the enterprise) are related to the general environment.

The social partners have begun to develop activities concerning the environment which fall into three main categories: *(a)* technical problems and research; *(b)* information and education of their members and of the public; and *(c)* consultations with public authorities and community groups in order to keep them informed and to influence standard-setting activities. Many employers' and workers' organisations have already established special machinery for activities related to the environment in order to support their members and to engage in joint consultation and negotiation. The mandate of enterprise-level health and safety committees could be broadened to include general environmental issues.

As understanding of the connection between the working and general environment has grown, these issues have come to be included in collective agreements and the scope of joint and tripartite collaboration has been extended.

In January 1989, the Federation of Netherlands Industry (VNO) and the Federation of Netherlands Trade Unions (FNV) adopted a Joint Statement on Environmental Policy based on their common concern for the environment, durable economic growth and employment. It was agreed that the increasing involvement of employers and workers in environmental issues should result in consultations between the parties at the level of industrial branches. This has been followed up by specific agreements at sectoral and enterprise levels concerning the role of employers in defining the environmental policy at enterprise level.

The possible inclusion of "green clauses" in collective agreements might deal, among other things, with the right of workers and their representatives *(a)* to be consulted in the elaboration of an environmental policy for the enterprise, based on the potential environmental hazard in its production processes or products; *(b)* to have access to unpublished information on environmental hazards and performance; *(c)* to participate in environmental audits/inspections of plants to evaluate environmental performance; *(d)* to provide training for workers' safety/environment delegates on environmental matters; *(e)* to refuse to undertake work which they believe might lead to serious pollution problems; *(f)* to receive advice from independent experts on environmental issues; *(g)* to invite the governmental environmental protection agency to inspect the plant.

In view of the possible employment and social repercussions of environment-related structural changes in industry, which may affect levels and locations of employment, industrial relations mechanisms will play an important role in ensuring that appropriate assistance is provided for workers affected by these changes, or for whom special environmental action may be required to protect their employment or who require re-training and adjustment help. Furthermore, possible new employment opportunities, related to environmental activities and "low-waste" technologies, may require significant changes in work practices and skills which may also become a subject of consultation between trade unions and employers.

Workers' and employers' organisations will increasingly be expected to look beyond the short-run economic issues to a perspective of sustainable economic growth, employment security and enhanced quality of work and life in the years to come.

Notes

[1] Rolf-Ulrich Sprenger: "Pollution control programmes and employment" in *IFO Digest,* 1/84.

[2] OECD: *Environment and economics,* results of the International Conference on Environment and Economics, 18-21 June 1984 (Paris, 1985), p. 93.

[3] loc. cit.

[4] *The role of the Community in implementing employment-related environmental measures,* final report, Vol. 1 (shortened version), prepared by W. Meissner and N. Lee (Oct. 1984), p. 5.

[5] ILO: *Employment and training implications of environmental policies in Europe,* document prepared for the Tripartite Meeting of Experts (Geneva, 29 Nov.-5 Dec. 1989) (doc. ETIEPE/1989/1).

[6] ILO: *Report of the Tripartite Meeting of Experts on Employment and Training Implications of Environmental Policies in Europe* (Geneva, 29 Nov.-5 Dec. 1989) (doc ETIEPE/1989/3).

[7] Vivian T. Sheridan: "Social impact of CFC phase-out", Du Pont de Nemours International, Geneva, 1989.

[8] *Our common future,* report of the World Commission on Environment and Development (the Brundtland Report) (Oxford, OUP, 1987), pp. 3, 8, 54, 248 and 249.

[9] Iftikhar Ahmed: "The bio-revolution in agriculture: Key to poverty alleviation in the Third World?" in *International Labour Review,* Vol. 127, No. 1, 1988.

[10] *The African Women's Assembly: Women and sustainable development,* by D. Loudiyi, B. Nagle and W. Ofosu-Amaah, a WorldWIDE publication.

[11] WHO: *Biomass fuel combustion and health,* doc. EFP/84.64 (Geneva 1984).

[12] ILO: *Safety in the working environment,* General Survey of the Reports on the Guarding of Machinery Convention (No. 119) and Recommendation (No. 118), 1963, and on the Working Environment (Air Pollution, Noise and Vibration) Convention (No. 148) and Recommendation (No. 156), 1977, Report III (Part 4 B), International Labour Conference, 73rd Session, Geneva, 1987.

[13] *ILO contribution to environmentally sound and sustainable development,* doc. GB.242/10/6/3, Geneva, Feb.-March 1989, para. 11.

[14] Nordic Council of Ministers: *Nordic programme for the environment* (Copenhagen, 1989), p. 46.

ROLE OF THE ILO's TRIPARTITE CONSTITUENTS

4

GOVERNMENTS AND THE ENVIRONMENT

This section will not attempt to review the full range of government responsibilities for the environment but will focus rather on the potential role of ministries of labour and employment, those most closely involved with the work of the ILO.

Until recently, the role of these ministries in respect of the environment was almost exclusively confined to occupational safety and health and the working environment. As environmental problems and policies have risen to the top of the political and public agenda, however, their potential impact on issues which fall specifically within the mandate of these ministries may be expected to increase. So far little study appears to have been made of the extent of this impact on labour and social issues. While some might suggest that this is because of the insignificance of the impact, it is more likely that such comments reflect a false sense of security, since so little thought has been given to the matter.

Ministries of labour and employment should monitor and examine such impacts more closely in future and, if appropriate, should also play a more active role within their governments' environment and development policy machinery so as to ensure that implications for the world of work—both positive and negative—are taken into account at all levels of the policy-making process. Environmental problems call for a co-ordinated, multidisciplinary approach so as to avoid isolated and contradictory policies and strategies. Ministries of labour and employment should play a limited, but vital, role here by drawing attention to potential labour and social implications and helping to reflect the views of employers' and workers' organisations. But beyond the review of impacts, when negative implications of environmental policies are identified these ministries should promote and implement appropriate "safety-net" measures to protect employers and workers affected by plant closures or major environment-driven structural adjustment. Above all, ministries of labour and employment must hold themselves ready to seize the many opportunities for expanded tripartite collaboration in respect of the environment so as to play their full part in the relevant activities.

Ministries of labour and employment, which often have responsibility for labour inspection activities, should also strengthen their activities and facilitate closer collaboration with other inspectorates responsible for general environmental issues. In some countries it may even be appropriate to consider the possibility of labour inspectorates being given additional responsibilities for some environmental monitoring and control, particularly in relation to industrial enterprises. Such co-ordination and collaboration would have very positive results for the working and general environment and lead to the more efficient use of limited resources.

As noted earlier, environmental investments and regulations will require significant training and retraining efforts in many sectors of the economy, including within governments. Ministries of labour and employment may be able to provide useful support for the assessment of manpower planning and training needs. Once critical skill shortages have been identified, ministries may also be able to promote a co-ordinated approach to the provision of training at all levels, within enterprises (formal and on-the-job training) and local communities as well as regionally and nationally.

In addition to specific vocational and management skills, however, these ministries should encourage training institutions to integrate environmental considerations into all vocational and management training programmes. This would have practical and cost-effective implications for environmental protection in the future.

Another important area in which these ministries may be able to contribute to environmental goals is by incorporating in general environmental awareness in public service training as well as in inspection and monitoring services. One of the most important factors for the future will be the capacity of governments to monitor and enforce environmental legislation, standards and guide-lines. This will no doubt require new technologies and new administrative and management initiatives, all of which will need to be reinforced through training and adequate technical and management support staff. As many governments are facing severe financial constraints, and some are even exploring new approaches such as the privatisation and subcontracting of some inspection services, the enforcement of such regulations is likely to be difficult.

Another issue which may affect some countries is the optimisation of environmental investments. Given the varying stages of development and level of technology from one country to another or between regions, a set level of investment in pollution control to protect a specific city or country might well be more efficiently invested in a neighbouring country since more would be achieved in terms of environmental quality if the money were spent on pollution control outside the country so as to decrease transboundary pollution. Such policy dilemmas will no doubt lead to a number of diplomatic challenges as well as opportunities. Nevertheless, such investments might lead to a shift of employment possibilities from one country to another, which might create opposition within the country financing the investment. Tripartite collaboration in such instances may no doubt be useful to smooth the way to a more effective use of environmental investments.

Governments will also need to play a very active role in the achievement of sustainable development and the alleviation of poverty. While in the past not all ministries of labour and employment have played a central role in the exchange of technical co-operation and bilateral assistance, there may be opportunities for them to collaborate more closely in the future—to share experience, for example, in such fields as the development of vocational and management training policies and centres; training and support related to strengthening labour inspection services; and, in particular, occupational safety and health issues such as hazardous chemicals and the risk of industrial accidents, as well as the setting up of emergency preparedness plans. All these activities—and no doubt many others which would be appropriate for these ministries—could do much to promote sustainable development.

EMPLOYERS' ORGANISATIONS AND THE ENVIRONMENT

Employers and their organisations have become key partners in the growing effort to protect and rehabilitate the environment. More and more companies are adopting explicit environmental policies and strategies which involve massive investments in pollution abatement equipment and the integration of new "clean" technologies and processes. In addition to new investments in equipment, however, there is a growing recognition of and management involvement in what has been called "corporate environmentalism".[1] The term describes the recognition by the highest level of management that corporate attitudes and performance in respect of the environment are now a fundamental factor in business success.

There are many different reasons motivating this new environmental awareness, including (a) the development of strong and active public interest in and support for environmental protection; (b) the rapid extension of legislation, standards and guide-lines at the national and local level which affect both the working and general environment; (c) the development of new business opportunities created by this public concern (e.g. new "green" products) and the passing of new legislation (laws on pollution abatement equipment and "clean" technologies); (d) the fear of economic constraints resulting from inefficient legislation which has motivated voluntary actions to remedy environmental problems before formal requirements are established; *(e)* the concern that recent major industrial accidents and incidents have created a very negative public image as well, in some countries, as the risk of sky-rocketing insurance costs and potentially costly liability claims; *(f)* the growing regional and international concern for the environment which has led to the prospect of new agreements, standards and guide-lines, and *(g)* increased recognition that all the above factors may also have a significant influence on the overall competitiveness of enterprises and possibly lead to unfair environmental trade advantages or constraints.

All these factors—and undoubtedly there are many more —clearly indicate that employers have an important stake in environmental policies. Consequently, they should also have a say in the development and implementation of those policies. The key question is how they can best ensure that their special contribution is effectively reflected in the policy-making process.

So far, employers and their organisations have been actively involved in environmental policies at the national and local levels. Furthermore, they provide the basis for economic growth and development which are essential to finance the new investments in environmental protection and rehabilitation. In addition, most of the vital research and development necessary for environmental regulations and standards—in the workplace and for the general environment—to have a firm scientific and technical basis have been financed by employers and their organisations who are, furthermore, the most important source for the development of new technologies—especially clean, low-waste and energy-efficient technologies.

Nevertheless, there is yet much to be done—and employers are increasingly devoting very significant proportions of their new investments and operating costs to environment-related activities, including the introduction of new tools such as environmental impact assessments for new investments and projects, and particularly the siting of new facilities; environmental auditing procedures; incentives for improved management through training; and special incentive payments and awards which recognise environmental performance and longer-term planning as well as short-term economic results.

In order to implement effectively the various environmental policies being developed by enterprises, employers' organisations and industry associations, the close collaboration of well-trained and environmentally aware employees is essential and may provide new opportunities for closer collaboration on the environment between employers and workers in the future.

Employers and their organisations are actively involved in environmental issues at all levels from the enterprise to international forums like the ILO. Industry associations representing specific sectors such as petroleum (e.g. International Petroleum Industry Environmental Conservation Association (IPIECA)) and chemicals (European Council of Chemical Manufacturers' Federations (CEFIC)) appear to be particularly involved, given the obvious connection between their activities and the environment. For example, the most recent annual consultative meeting organised by the UNEP Industry and Environment Office in Paris with trade/industry associations attracted 12 sectoral organisations and a large number of national industry associations. The International Chamber of Commerce (ICC), for example, is very actively involved in environmental issues and, following the World Industry Conference on Environmental Management (organised by UNEP and the ICC in 1984), created an International Environment Bureau to serve as an international clearing-house for environmental management information. The ICC has also a Commission on Environment which has prepared Guidelines for World Industry, as well as a position paper on Environmental Auditing.

Since 1984 the ILO, in close collaboration with UNEP and with the support of the International Organisation of Employers, has been implementing a special programme on environmental training and awareness for employers' organisations. Regional employers' meetings on environment (including the working environment) and development were convened for the Asia and Pacific Region (1984),

English-speaking Africa, French-speaking Africa (1985) and Latin America (1987). They have been followed up by a series of national seminars and support activities in 16 developing countries.

These meetings have highlighted a number of areas, indicated hereafter, in which employers' organisations may be able to play a useful role.

— *Environmental legislation:* They should seek to be consulted on a regular basis in the drafting of environmental laws, regulations and standards, as well as the modalities of their application.

— *Environmentally sound technologies:* They should provide a clearing-house service for their members concerning environmental technologies, centralising access to international information networks.

— *Environmental awareness:* They should promote environmental awareness among their members through information, education and training.

— *Training:* They should integrate general environmental training, especially for managers, within their traditional training activities.

— *Exchange of information:* They should facilitate the exchange of relevant information both between members and with other employers' organisations, regionally and internationally.

Increasingly, employers and their organisations also recognise that they have an important role to play in implementing the broader concept of sustainable development. Employers and their organisations have the opportunity to facilitate international exchanges of information, technologies and expertise among themselves.

WORKERS' ORGANISATIONS AND THE ENVIRONMENT

In addition to all their other roles and responsibilities, workers and their organisations are also "environmental" organisations by virtue of the extremely high priority they have given to the protection of the working environment. The traditional view that the working environment existed in total isolation to the general environment has been replaced, particularly in workers' circles, by recognition that the two are closely interlinked.

But this increasing awareness on the part of the workers is not only a matter of changing perceptions but also involves their traditional and growing concern about issues related to conditions of life such as housing, transport, the availability of food, water and sanitation facilities, educational opportunities, leisure and recreation. Furthermore, the workers' attitudes have also been influenced by the relatively recent realisation that past predictions of plant closures and economic disruption, expected to result from environmental protection policies, have simply not proved correct. Today, many believe that environmental policies—if properly formulated and implemented over an appropriate time period—can also lead to new employment opportunities. At the same time, the awareness of environmental challenges facing our planet has also led to an understanding that environmentally unsound jobs will not be sustainable and that action needs to be taken now to ensure that sustainable employment is created and protected. Workers also realise, however, that when employment is threatened by necessary environmental action, the costs should be borne not only by the workers directly concerned but shared by society, which in any case will benefit from an improved environment. Therefore, workers and their organisations are demanding equitable support and adjustment measures to provide assistance for those who lose employment in the form of retraining, placement and relocation, and other "safety-net" measures. Workers have also drawn attention to the impact on communities, where secondary and tertiary employment is also often affected and solidarity and special assistance may also be required. To a community which has lost its economic lifeline, a cleaner environment becomes a poisoned fruit.

As a result of these changing attitudes and policies, workers and their organisations have become increasingly involved in general environment issues at the enterprise level, as well as through their national, regional, international and sector-based organisations.

While it is not possible in this Report to provide an in-depth review of the wide range of environmental issues directly and indirectly affecting workers and their organisations, it may nevertheless be useful to provide an incomplete—but still impressive—list of activities and potential roles for workers and their organisations at the enterprise level:

— given their day-to-day experience in the workplace, workers and their organisations can make an important contribution to the improvement of the working and general environment and should make a point of ensuring that they are informed and consulted at an early stage on all environment questions;

— the active involvement of workers and their organisations should be sought concerning the design and implementation of all environmental policies or programmes which might promote new employment, protect existing employment, or lead to the loss of employment (with the consequent need to institute adequate "safety-net" measures);

— workers need access to information on—if not actual participation in—the establishment of company environmental strategies or policies; the introduction of new technologies; monitoring of chemical emissions inside and outside the plant; environmental audits; inspections and reports regarding compliance with environmental regulations and standards, etc.; in other words, they need "the right to know";

— workers should participate in the design and development of training programmes for workers and management to provide environmental awareness and the skills necessary to meet environmental objectives; special efforts should be made to ensure that workers' health-and-safety representatives or special environmental representatives receive appropriate environmental training;

— workers should promote the setting up of special joint committees to deal with general environment issues or the broadening of the mandate of existing joint committees (e.g. health and safety committees) to encompass the general environment;

— workers should consider the creation of special trade union environmental committees, if appropriate;

— workers should actively participate in environmental activities within the local community, and facilitate exchanges of views on potential problems and activities of common concern;

— workers may be able to influence the purchasing policies of enterprises, consumers and governments in order to identify and promote products which are safe for the working and general environment, by such means as the establishment of standards on environmental certification or labelling;

— workers should urge employers to recognise good environmental performance by workers and management and to provide incentives for such performance;

— workers should co-operate with appropriate government inspection authorities to ensure the improvement and enforcement of regulations and standards on the working and general environment;

— workers should collaborate with employers, governments and consumers to ensure that the "polluter pays principle" is enforced and that the costs are not simply passed on to consumers without the polluter making investments to prevent further pollution.

In addition to these possible activities at the enterprise level, it may be useful to recall the number of collective bargaining issues mentioned earlier (Chapter 3, in the section on industrial relations) which will, of course, also be important objectives and activities for many workers and their organisations at the enterprise level.

Many of these same activities and roles at the enterprise level will also be relevant for national, regional and international workers' organisations, which will need to strengthen their capacity to provide support, including information, training and advice, to workers and their organisations at the enterprise level.

A number of additional activities are also being considered by national, regional and international workers' organisations, for example:

— active involvement in the development and implementation of environmental legislation, standards, codes of practice and guidelines at all levels;

— research into and analysis of the implications of environment on the world of work and wide dissemination of the results;

— the general exchange of information and experience on environment and the world of work as well as advance warning of new potential hazards or problems related to the working and general environment;

— making national, regional and international policy-makers aware of the positive and negative implications of environmental policies and problems for workers and actively participating in the policy-making process, particularly by identifying and promoting practical and effective measures to accentuate the positive and mitigate or eliminate the negative impacts.

Trade union solidarity with workers throughout the world who are struggling to overcome extreme poverty and injustice is constantly challenging workers' organisations everywhere to support the achievement of sustainable development. Workers' organisations may be able to promote and contribute to new opportunities to strengthen and deepen the process of North-South, East-West and

South-South collaboration related to the environment and sustainable development.

OPPORTUNITIES FOR TRIPARTITE COLLABORATION

Environmental problems and policies will provide many new challenges and opportunities for tripartite collaboration.[2] The joint statement on environmental policy by the Federation of Netherlands Industry (VNO) and the Federation of Netherlands Trade Unions (FNV) provides a useful review of possible areas of collaboration:

It is the government's task to state the aims and methods of environmental policy and to ensure that the necessary funds are obtained as far as possible from the proceeds of economic growth.

It is the task of the central organisations of employers and employees to contribute to the formulation of these policy aims and to encourage their members to take action to fulfil them.

It is also the responsibility of the central organisations to ensure that environmental protection measures are effective in an international context and that their social and economic consequences are acceptable.

Tripartite collaboration plays a crucial role in many vital areas of economic and social policy and environmental issues have been given a major place on the new agenda. This Report has referred to a wide range of environmental issues, all with potential employment and social implications. As stated earlier, the problems of the environment are not so much technical as political, economic and social. Some of these issues may therefore be very appropriate subjects for tripartite consultation within the context of the ILO's Tripartite Consultation (International Labour Standards) Convention, 1976 (No. 144), and Tripartite Consultation (Activities of the International Labour Organisation) Recommendation, 1976 (No. 152). Tripartite collaboration is particularly appropriate to help seek consensus on the replies to the following critical questions: What should be done about the environment? By whom? Who should pay? Who will enforce what is decided? Without the active participation and collaboration of governments and the social partners, it will be impossible to achieve our sustainable development objectives. All three partners need to be more aware of the challenges confronting our planet. We shall need to create a new acceptance of collaboration in respect of the environment and avoid the past focus on confrontation. We need to prevent the polarisation of positions and to seek new and innovative solutions. To do this the social partners must talk together, listen to others and seek a constructive and practical consensus.

Given the immense costs required to achieve environmental and sustainable development objectives, it will not be possible to do everything at once. The process of setting priorities, using natural resources in the most efficient and effective manner possible, and ensuring an equitable sharing of costs and benefits will require tripartite collaboration, consensus and international solidarity.

There are several special areas which appear to be particularly ripe for new tripartite initiatives. For example, although the search for solutions to global warming is at present constrained by scientific uncertainty, there are many policies that make good sense, both economically and environmentally, regardless of further scientific verification of climate change. Energy efficiency and conservation and improved transport systems are the two most important. In both these sectors a tripartite approach is not only feasible but highly necessary. Governments will need to establish new energy and transport strategies and standards in collaboration with employers, workers and the general public; industry must invest in research and development and the production of energy-efficient equipment, new sources of energy, and transport systems and vehicles to meet these objectives; and the workers hold the key to the successful implementation of the production adjustments required, as well as to their acceptance by society.

In the United Kingdom, for example, the Confederation of British Industry has endorsed a major campaign to encourage its members to implement practical energy-conservation guide-lines in order to help control the greenhouse effect. Many workers' organisations are also actively involved in campaigns to encourage energy-efficiency programmes. In such cases, special benefits would be derived from joint programmes or activities between governments and employers' and workers' organisations. Such collaboration could make a major contribution to overall awareness by the public of the important environmental challenges facing us and how we all must work together to meet them.

One of the most important areas for tripartite collaboration related to the environment is the continued strengthening of existing tripartite activities to improve the working environment. As noted earlier, direct preventive action at the workplace where the problems are created would be one of the most efficient ways of reducing potentially harmful effects on the general environment.

As the environmental agenda continues to expand, no doubt many new problems which will also affect labour and social conditions will appear. We therefore need to be flexible in our approach and ready for surprises. One of the characteristics of humanity for centuries has been its capacity to adapt; some now suggest that we are losing that capacity. The environmental challenge will put our ability to adapt to the test. Successful adaptation in today's society will require close collaboration between all segments of society so that we not only adapt to change, but do so from the perspective of social justice and equity.

Notes

[1] *Corporate environmentalism,* statement by E. S. Woolard, Chairman of E. I. Du Pont de Nemours and Company, before the American Chamber of Commerce (UK), London, 4 May 1989.

[2] See also *Working for a better environment: The role of the social partners,* report on a round table meeting organised by the European Foundation for the Improvement of Living and Working Conditions, Dublin, 8-10 June 1988, Information Booklet Series No. 13 (Luxembourg, Office for Official Publications of the European Communities, 1989).

ROLE OF THE INTERNATIONAL
LABOUR ORGANISATION AND OFFICE $\quad$ 5

Given the magnitude and scope of environmental activities in the future, and the fact that the entire United Nations system and other international organisations are also mobilised to contribute to environmentally sound and sustainable development, it is essential for the ILO to carefully establish priorities for its own role and contribution. In the light of financial constraints and concern that environmental issues might deflect the ILO from other equally or even more important labour and social priorities also demanding more attention, it will be necessary to select those activities in which the Organisation and the Office have a unique and clear comparative advantage.

Annex I to this Report, entitled *ILO contribution to environmentally sound and sustainable development*, which was submitted to the 44th Session of the United Nations General Assembly by the Governing Body, provides a review of the ILO's past activities related to these issues as well as an indication of possible new areas of concern and action for the future. However, a number of additional environmental issues have been raised within this Conference Report which indicate further areas for possible action by the Organisation and the Office.

Despite the wide range of issues raised in this Report, however, the most important role for the Office appears to be to support its tripartite constituents so that they themselves can deal directly with them. Although environmental problems are increasingly and correctly seen as creating regional and global implications, solutions to these problems will need to be found and implemented primarily at the local level. Of course, policies and strategies must be developed at the national, regional and international level to ensure a co-ordinated and integrated approach, but the actual decisions on investment, changes in technologies, restructuring of production processes, employment, training and work procedures, etc., will have to take place at the enterprise level.

Consequently, the Office has already set as one of its major environmental priorities the strengthening of employers' and workers' organisations so that they can deal more effectively with these issues themselves. The successful ILO/UNEP programme to support environmental activities within employers' organisations at the regional and national level will be strengthened and expanded. Thanks to a major contribution by the Government of Norway, a similar programme of training and institutional support concerning the environment is about to be launched for workers' organisations throughout the world. This specific activity will reinforce the ongoing activities of the Workers' Education Programme aimed at integrating environmental considerations within many of its traditional training programmes. By targeting its support efforts upon the social partners, the ILO will be able to make a major contribution to environment and development in an area clearly within its mandate and in which it has a unique comparative advantage. In future, it may even be appropriate for the Office to promote and support a series of national tripartite environmental seminars to facilitate the development of tripartite collaboration at the national level.

Another priority role for the Organisation and the Office is to take advantage of their unique tripartite international perspective to draw attention to problems which may affect labour and social conditions in the coming decades. I hope that this Report will create a greater awareness and understanding of potential implications for the world of work that will enable the ILO's constituents to take action at an early stage, thereby avoiding problems and promoting new opportunities. The discussion at the Conference is likely to provide a lively and controversial exchange of views and opinions on environmental risks and priorities, and possible policy responses. This will no doubt generate another important role for the ILO: the exchange of information and experience concerning environment and the world of work. The outcome of the research being carried out at all levels will need to be broadly disseminated so as to prevent duplication and to ensure that we learn from each other's successes and failures.

In addition to these special activities, the ILO need to strengthen its efforts to integrate the question of the environment and sustainable development within its mainstream programmes.

In order to support the development of environmental education and training, the Office is developing a new environmental training strategy, which will be finalised following the Conference discussion. Several issues are important, such as training programmes directed at anticipatory and preventive activities. In addition to the programmes already mentioned for employers' and workers' organisations, the ILO should also devote more effort to integrating appropriate environmental considerations in the training activities related to other ILO programmes, for example at the Turin Centre and the International Institute for Labour Studies, as well as in the training activities for co-operatives, rural development, labour-intensive infrastructure projects, employment and appropriate technology, occupational safety and health and conditions of work and life.

The ILO will also need to collaborate closely with other organisations active in the area of environmental training. As stated above, the Office is already co-operating with UNEP and has established direct technical contacts with UNESCO, UNDP, OECD, the Commission of the European Communities and others. In particular, the Office will expand its collaboration with the UNESCO/UNEP International Environmental Education Programme and with multi-bilateral development agencies.

One of the keys to the ILO's success over the past 71 years has been its system of international labour standards. The Organisation provides a universal, tripartite forum for the development of standards and specific procedures to monitor their application. Very useful lessons may be gained from the ILO's experience in the field of international standards which would be directly applicable to the future development of environmental standards. The Office will make a special effort to share its experience with UNEP and others with a view to offering practical assistance in the development of international environmental standards.

At the same time, the International Labour Organisation itself could develop new international standards, particularly as regards the working environment (e.g. standards on the prevention of major industrial hazards). Several of the ILO's existing standards—such as those related to the working environment and to indigenous and tribal peoples—already contain provisions on general environmental conditions and due attention should be given to the need to protect the general environment when formulating new standards. It is also important that these standards should not be incompatible with those being adopted in other international forums.

Furthermore, the Organisation should encourage the ratification and effective implementation of ILO standards, especially those related to the working environment. The Office for its part should reinforce its efforts to link international standards to technical cooperation and expand its assistance to developing countries to help them to implement ratified Conventions and to meet their constitutional obligations, particularly as regards the working environment.

The Office may also need to reinforce its efforts aimed at the alleviation of poverty, with special emphasis on activities which meet developing countries' own special environmental priorities. Such activities are likely to be the most direct, urgent and practical contribution the ILO can make to sustainable development. This is particularly evident in the ILO's labour-intensive activities to develop environment-related infrastructures (e.g. afforestation, irrigation, flood protection and land rehabilitation). The ILO's activities related to rural development, especially those designed to provide assistance to particularly vulnerable groups, such as women and indigenous and tribal populations, provide an important opportunity to promote environmentally sound and sustainable development. Furthermore, the

ILO's programmes directed at the development and support of the informal sector in urban areas of developing countries as well as its activities related to technologies and employment should also integrate practical environmental considerations within their activities.

The Office will need to step up its efforts to collect and analyse information concerning the relationship between employment and the environment. In this context, it may even be appropriate to establish a special ad hoc multidisciplinary research team to analyse the potential employment and training effects of environmental problems and policies currently under discussion, such as global climate change and the prevention of ozone depletion. Such research might provide a useful contribution to the present international policy-making and implementation process, as well as supporting activities of the ILO's constituents at the national level.

As regards the working environment, many opportunities exist for the Office to strengthen its major programme of activities within the Working Conditions and Environment Department, especially within the framework of the International Programme for the Improvement of Working Conditions and Environment (PIACT). Particular emphasis might be placed on the following:

— activities to strengthen the management of occupational safety and health, especially with regard to hazards that may seriously affect both the working and the general environment;

— activities related to major hazard control, e.g. preparation of a code of practice, expanded technical co-operation activities, and the possible development of international instruments concerning major hazard control;

— information dissemination activities such as the ILO's International Occupational Safety and Health Information Centre (CIS), the ILO's International Registry of Chemical Safety Information Sheets (IRCIS), and the ILO's International Occupational Safety and Health Hazard Alert System;

— as a follow-up to the resolution concerning harmonisation of systems of classification and labelling for the use of hazardous chemicals at work, adopted by the International Labour Conference at its 76th Session, the ILO is beginning to harmonise the criteria and system of classification and labelling of chemicals at work in close collaboration with UNEP and the WHO through the IPCS.

As environmental problems and policies will have special implications in many of the sectors covered by the ILO's Programme of Sectoral Activities, Industrial and analogous Committees, tripartite technical meetings and meetings of experts could provide a useful forum for a detailed examination of sector-specific environmental impacts on the world of work. Several of these committees have in the past examined environmental aspects and adopted resolutions (e.g. Chemical Industries Committee at its Tenth Session in 1988). This may be particularly relevant for sectors which are expected to undergo extensive restructuring as a result of environmental and other factors, for example transport (air pollution, control of CO_2 and other greenhouse gases); the chemical industries (prevention of industrial hazards, impact of bans on hazardous chemicals); the coal mining and petroleum industries (control of CO_2 emissions and air pollution); fisheries (effects of the depletion of fish stocks); and forestry (effects of pollution and policies related to protection of forests).

Such tripartite sectoral approaches to environmental issues of particular importance to key sectors may become increasingly important in future in identifying collaborative tripartite approaches to the related labour and social issues at the local, national, regional and international levels.

In carrying out these various environment-related activities, special emphasis will also be given to ensuring that the ILO does not work in isolation but improves its collaboration with the United Nations system and with other international and regional institutions concerned with the environment. The ILO's specific mandate concerning the working environment will require the Office to play an active and dynamic leadership role concerning these issues both within and outside the United Nations system. The ILO's special tripartite structure also provides a unique opportunity for the Office to reflect the special views and priorities of the social partners within other international forums. As these other organisations and institutions will play the most important and direct role concerning the environment, the ILO should reflect the views and consensus of the social partners so that they are taken into account when environmental problems and new policy solutions are discussed elsewhere. At the same time, the ILO itself should take more advantage of the work being carried out within the United Nations system and other institutions and facilitate the dissemination of relevant information to the social partners to help support their environmental activities. The ILO will continue its active role within the special mechanism of the Administrative Committee on Co-ordination for inter-agency co-operation on the environment called the Designated Officials for Environmental Matters (DOEM) as well as the System-Wide Medium-Term Environment Programme (SWMTEP).

Finally, the preparatory process for the proposed United Nations Conference on Environment and Development in 1992 will provide an excellent opportunity for the ILO to draw attention to the views, concerns and proposals concerning environment and the world of work made by tripartite delegations during the Conference discussion. At the same time, the Office will need to ensure that the United Nations Conference is kept informed of the special interests and activities of employers' and workers' organisations and of the need for the social partners to have an opportunity to collaborate in the policy-making process and the implementation of any future plan of action.

CONCLUSIONS

One of the objectives of this Report has been to urge the ILO's tripartite partners to reflect upon environmental issues at an early stage and to ensure that action is taken, where necessary, to prevent them from combining into a "critical mass" which could lead to labour and social repercussions of sufficient magnitude as to prevent or delay necessary action or even lead to serious social conflict.

My purpose has been to pose a number of questions to the Conference's tripartite delegations in order to challenge them to reflect on these issues and to make them aware of the potential implications in their own specific fields of concern and responsibility. In addition, I have pointed out a number of areas in which the International Labour Organisation and Office might play a useful role. It is clear that the ILO cannot—and should not try to—deal with all the issues raised in this Report concerning environment and the world of work. Clearly, some issues are more important than others, some are more amenable to international action than others, and some may be more "ripe" for intervention now or in the near future while others must await further scientific information or political consensus. I look to the Conference to provide clear guidance as to which issues and activities should receive priority from the Organisation and Office in the future, particularly during the period of the next Programme and Budget, 1992-93.

When I selected the theme of environment and the world of work, I was fully aware that it would not be possible to prepare a definitive description of the effects environmental problems and policies might have on employment, training, the working environment and other labour and social situations. Nevertheless, given the rapid changes taking place in environmental policy, it is important that these issues be raised now and not later. I remain convinced that ministries of labour and employment, and employers' and workers' organisations, have a special role to play in this policy-making process and—what is even more important—in the process of making those policies work.

I look forward to your participation in the Conference discussion which, in addition to providing the ILO's tripartite partners with an opportunity to express their views concerning environment and development, will also set the Office's environment and development agenda for the next decade.

ILO CONTRIBUTION TO ENVIRONMENTALLY SOUND AND SUSTAINABLE DEVELOPMENT

Report of the Governing Body of the International Labour Office to the 44th Session of the General Assembly in response to General Assembly resolutions 42/186 and 42/187

INTRODUCTION

1. The ILO Governing Body has given increasing attention to matters relating to environment and development since its session in February-March 1988 when it was first informed of the Report of the World Commission on Environment and Development entitled: *Our common future* and the Environmental Perspective to the Year 2000 and Beyond. At its 242nd Session, the Governing Body examined a paper submitted by the Director-General which had a twofold purpose. First, it provided a review of the ILO's past and present activities related to environmentally sound and sustainable development with a view to receiving comments and guidance from the Governing Body on future priorities and activities in this field. Secondly, after being revised to take into account the Governing Body's comments, this paper is now being submitted as the official ILO response to the requests contained in General Assembly resolutions 42/186 (environmental Perspective to the Year 2000 and Beyond) and 42/187 (report of the World Commission on Environment and Development) which ask the Governing Body of the ILO (like the governing bodies of other organisations) to report to the General Assembly at its 44th Session, through the Economic and Social Council, on progress made in the ILO towards environmentally sound and sustainable development. This paper is also being made available to the Governing Council of the United Nations Environment Programme at its 15th Session in May 1989.

THE ILO AND ENVIRONMENTALLY SOUND
AND SUSTAINABLE DEVELOPMENT

2. Before reviewing ILO activities, it may be useful to define how the office has interpreted the concept of environmentally sound and sustainable development. The Environmental Perspective to the Year 2000 and Beyond was prepared by UNEP and adopted by the UNEP Governing Council and the General Assembly in 1987. It was adopted as a "broad framework to guide national action and international co-operation on policies and programmes aimed at achieving environmentally sound and sustainable development, and specifically as a guide to the preparation of further system-wide medium-term environment programmes and the medium-term programmes of the organisations and bodies of the United Nations system". Resolution 42/186 also provides a review of the "perceptions shared by governments of the nature of environmental problems, and their inter-relations with other international problems, and of the efforts to deal with them". The Environmental Perspective reflects many of the concerns contained on the report of the World Commission on Environment and Development (WCED).

3. The report of the WCED entitled *Our common future,* and also known as the Brundtland Report after the Commission's Chairman, Mrs. Gro Harlem Brundtland, now Prime Minister of Norway, sets forth the fundamental idea that economic and social development should be based on the concept of "sustainable development", that is "development that meets the needs of the present without compromising the ability of future generations to meet their own needs". The Commission's report defines a number of concepts or perspectives in connection with the process of sustainable development: *time,* i.e. present and future generations; *needs,* especially meeting the basic needs of the world's poor; the *limitations* of technology and social organisation; *equity,* within and between countries; *integrated approaches* to policies and actions; *natural resource management; anticipation* and *prevention* as well as *rehabilitation.* The challenge facing the ILO and others is to implement this concept of sustainable development in its day-to-day activities.

4. Taking into account the all-embracing nature of the concept, the Director-General noted in his remarks at the Oslo Conference on Sustainable Development in July 1988 that "*every* ILO activity–and no doubt this is true of all our UN agencies and entities–is directed, in principle, to the achievement of sustainable development". The Director-General requested an interdepartmental review of the Brundtland Report and its implications for the ILO. The results of that review underlined how closely the ILO's activities, programmes and objectives are already interlinked with the concept of sustainable development. There are three areas of particular priority and concern for the ILO: the working environment, environmental

training and the relationships between environment and employment, poverty and development.

THE WORKING ENVIRONMENT

5. The working environment, which received relatively limited emphasis within the Brundtland Report and the Environmental Perspective, receives very high priority within the ILO. The ILO has a constitutional mandate to assist countries in improving their working environment and since 1919 has devoted a significant proportion of its efforts in that direction, especially through its standard-setting activities.

6. The high priority to be given to these issues was recently reiterated at the Seventh ILO African Regional Conference held in Harare in 1988 when it adopted a resolution concerning the protection of the working and general environment in the African region. It calls upon all member States and in particular those from that region and the Director-General to take various actions concerning a number of critical issues related to the working and general environment, including hazardous wastes. The extensive programmes carried out by the ILO in the field of occupational safety and health and conditions of work and life make a major contribution to environmentally sound and sustainable development. The Working Environment (Air Pollution, Noise and Vibration) Convention (No. 148), and Recommendation (No. 156), 1977, as well as the Safety and Health in Construction Convention (No. 167) and Recommendation (No. 175), adopted in June 1988, are examples of the ILO's contribution through international standards. A first discussion of safety in the use of chemicals at work, with a view to the adoption of an instrument or instruments, will take place at the International Labour Conference in June 1989.

7. In addition to standard-setting activities, various other activities are being carried out during the present biennium with the overall objective of promoting and supporting efforts at the international, regional and national levels to reduce occupational accidents and diseases and to improve the working environment. The work programme of the Occupational Safety and Health Branch within the Working Conditions and Environment Department has been developed with a view to achieving this long-term objective. These programme elements include: *(a)* the preparation of draft codes of practice on (i) safety and health in construction, (ii) safety and health in surface mining operations, and (iii) the prevention of major hazards; *(b)* a meeting of experts on safety in the use of mineral and synthetic fibres; *(c)* a study on the provision of occupational health services at the national level for small-scale enterprises, agricultural workers and the informal sector; *(d)* an inventory of occupational safety and health activities of employers' associations and trade

unions; *(e)* a training manual on the use of chemicals at work; and *(f)* dissemination of information through the ILO's International Occupational Safety and Health Information Centre (CIS) and the International Occupational Safety and Health Hazard Alert System.

8. In carrying out its activities concerning the working environment, the ILO collaborates actively with other international organisations, including other UN agencies, as well as non-governmental organisations. For example, action is being taken jointly with the International Social Security Association (ISSA) for the hosting of the 12th World Congress on Occupational Safety and Health in 1990. Inter-agency co-operation with the UNEP/WHO/ILO International Programme on Chemical Safety (IPCS)[1] and the IAEA continues to be strengthened for the protection of workers exposed to chemicals and radiation, respectively. The Seventh International Pneumoconiosis Conference held in August 1987 provided a forum for exchange of information on lung diseases, engineering and medical measures of protection of workers from dust diseases and other health hazards.

9. In addition to activities under the regular budget, the Office is carrying out a wide range of operational activities aimed at improving the working environment. These activities are part of the ILO's International Programme for the Improvement of Working Conditions and Environment, known as PIACT, which was established in 1976. Furthermore, extra-budgetary resources are available from the UNDP and other multi-bilateral donors for technical co-operation activities. Many of the technical co-operation projects are aimed at assisting governments in the formulation and implementation of national policies on occupational safety and health, in particular by improving the technical competence of occupational safety and health inspection services and strengthening national safety and health institutions. Some 20 projects of this kind are operational in developing countries. An important new subject is the establishment and operation of major hazard control systems in several countries in Asia. Projects on safety and health in mining are also operational in some countries. Another significant feature of several projects is the provision of advice and training to employers' and workers' representatives. An Asian regional project on occupational safety and health and workers' welfare in construction is also operational.

10. The Conditions of Work and Welfare Facilities Branch is carrying out many activities related to working time, work organisation, work content and technologies which are directly related to the working environment. In addition, work-related welfare facilities and services often also have an important influence upon the working environment; for example, inadequate housing, sanitation and transport facilities can affect the worker's health and safety on the job.

11. In a world of rapidly changing technologies and products, including new chemical substances and growing concern about hazardous wastes, issues related to

the working environment have become increasingly complex and more closely linked to the general environment. As a result, the past distinction between the working environment and the general environment has become less clear. Lasting solutions to the problems of the working environment can be found only in the broader context of the improvement of the general environment. Similarly, the problems of the general environment cannot be satisfactorily tackled unless the problems of the working environment are effectively solved. For example, monitoring and assessing permissible levels of exposure of workers to chemicals at the workplace may also need to take into account levels of exposure to other chemicals encountered by those workers outside the working environment. Recent industrial accidents, unfortunately, also have provided dramatic examples of the linkages between the working environment and the general environment. These linkages may require the ILO to co-ordinate its activities concerning the working environment more closely with the work of others dealing with the general environment.

12. The ILO's past activities concerning the working environment have given priority to industrial and other organised sectors of the economy. In future, increasing priority will need to be given to the working environment of workers in commercial establishments such as shops and offices (e.g. indoor air pollution), as well as workers in rural areas and the informal sector of developing countries. It should also be noted that, recognising the rapid increase in the world's population, millions of new jobs—and new working environments—will need to be created and the ILO's challenge will be to ensure that these jobs are safe, environmentally sound and sustainable.

ENVIRONMENTAL TRAINING

13. The ILO has undertaken environmental training activities in the framework of its traditional vocational training, management development, workers' education and employers' organisations training programmes as well as at the International Centre for Advanced Technical and Vocational Training in Turin and the International Institute for Labour Studies.[2] Although to date these activities have been limited, there appears to be considerable scope for expanding them within all types of national and regional training programmes supported by the ILO.

14. A useful example of the kind of special contribution the ILO can make to environmental training may be seen in the series of information and training activities launched by the Bureau for Employers' Activities. These activities are designed to make employers aware of the principles and practices of environmentally sound management and have been carried out in Asia, Africa and Latin America. This Programme, which has been carried out in close collaboration with UNEP, now also

provides for special national training seminars to strengthen the capacity of employers' organisations to implement their own national environmental training programmes.

15. Despite the specific environmental training activities already carried out by the ILO, the Office has not so far had a formal strategy on environmental training. Therefore, the Director-General has requested an interdepartmental working group to prepare such a strategy in the near future. It is particularly examining the specific role that the ILO might play in this field. Several issues appear to be especially important. For example, higher priority should be given to developing training programmes directed at anticipatory and preventive activities than to those dealing with rehabilitation and alleviation; special efforts are needed to develop a training programme for workers' organisations comparable to that devised for employers' organisations; and the ILO should develop special support activities to ensure that environmental specialists at the national and regional levels who are carrying out training activities are fully aware of general training issues and problems which might also be relevant in environmental training; in other words, environmental trainers should be helped to avoid making the same mistakes that occurred in the development and implementation of other training programmes. In addition, the ILO should devote more effort to integrating appropriate environmental issues within training activities related to other ILO programmes, e.g. co-operatives, rural development, labour-intensive public works projects, employment and technology projects, and activities related to occupational safety and health and conditions of work and life. Furthermore, the ILO, particularly in light of its tripartite structure, has an opportunity to play an active role in raising general environmental awareness.

16. The ILO will also need to collaborate more closely with other bodies working in the area of environmental training. The Office has already established direct technical contacts with UNEP, UNESCO, OECD, the Commission of the European Communities and others. It could make a particularly useful contribution to the UNESCO/UNEP International Environmental Education Programme as regards vocational and employers' and workers' training. In developing its strategy for environmental training, special attention will be given to ensuring that the ILO will play a unique and complementary role in this important field.

ENVIRONMENT AND EMPLOYMENT, POVERTY AND DEVELOPMENT

17. The Brundtland Report and the Environmental Perspective correctly emphasise that poverty is a major cause and effect of global environmental prob-

lems. As stated in the Commission's report: "A world in which poverty is endemic will always be prone to ecological and other crises". Activities aimed at alleviating poverty, creating employment and generating income activities are central to the ILO's technical co-operation programmes and advisory services. The ILO's policies, programmes and projects in these areas will need to be reinforced by integrating environmental and sustainable development considerations more effectively into them. The ILO has so far carried out many projects, especially in the context of its labour-intensive public works programmes, which have aimed at the rehabilitation or protection of the environment, for example wasteland development and land-reclamation projects, including irrigation and forestry-related activities. The dire prospects for rural employment suggest that new approaches will be required. The conclusions concerning rural employment promotion adopted by the International Labour Conference in June 1988 provide useful insights which complement the World Commission's Report.

18. The International Labour Conference in June 1989 is expected to complete its discussions concerning the partial revision of the Convention (No. 107) concerning the protection and integration of indigenous and other tribal and semi-tribal populations in independent countries, adopted in 1957 together with a Recommendation (No. 104) on the same subject. Recognising the emphasis given in the World Commission's Report to these populations and other vulnerable groups, the ILO has a unique opportunity, within its area of competence and in collaboration with others, to promote and support national action to help indigenous populations achieve environmentally sound and sustainable development.

19. The Director-General has drawn attention to the fact that very often *rural* and *urban* areas requiring environmental protection and rehabilitation in both *North* and *South* are also facing severe unemployment and poverty. This suggests that the ILO should respond in a more integrated fashion to both problems. The ILO should assist governments to ensure both that their environmental policies more effectively reflect employment requirements and opportunities and that their employment policies more effectively reflect environmental considerations. The Government of Norway has recently approved a special project concerning ILO action to support sustainable development, under which the Office will be able to carry out initial research on the inter-relationships between environment and employment. These activities will be supplemented by a special item in the Programme and Budget proposals for 1990-91.

MEETING OF EXPERTS

20. The Governing Body, at its 242nd Session in March 1989, decided to convene, particularly in response to the resolution on employment policy and environmental protection adopted at the Fourth ILO European Regional Conference in September 1987, a Tripartite Meeting of Experts on Employment and Training Implications of Environmental Policies in Europe (Geneva, 29 November-5 December 1989).

NEW AREAS OF CONCERN AND ACTION

21. The interdepartmental review of the Brundtland Report drew attention to a number of related activities which the ILO will need to undertake to integrate environmental and sustainable development considerations within its major technical programmes. Some of the most important factors mentioned in the Brundtland Report calling for reinforcement include the following:

(a) the design, implementation and evaluation of ILO programmes and projects should reflect a *longer-term perspective;*

(b) considering that the inequitable sharing of the social, economic and environmental costs and benefits of development cannot lead to sustainable development but only to continued poverty, injustice and division, *equity* should be one of the important criteria in the design, implementation and evaluation of ILO projects;

(c) the ILO should give special support to environmental activities providing an opportunity for *tripartite collaboration* and also should encourage others to take advantage of a tripartite approach in their activities;

(d) the ILO should continue to strengthen the *linkages between its technical co-operation activities and international labour standards* so as to assist developing countries to implement ratified Conventions, especially those concerned with the working environment;

(e) the ILO should give higher priority to the use of project "teams" which draw together expertise from more than one ILO technical unit, so as to ensure that projects reflect a more co-ordinated and *intergrated approach* to sustainable development;

(f) recognising the important environmental implications of many ILO projects, the Office should establish a practicable *environmental impact review process,* based on experience gained through the special environmental review activities proposed for the period 1989-91, so as to ensure that relevant projects and programmes adequately take into account environmental considerations;

(g) the Office should develop *internal staff training and advisory support activities* in order to assist ILO staff at headquarters and in the field to integrate environmental and sustainable development considerations more effectively in their traditional activities.

CO-ORDINATION WITHIN THE UNITED NATIONS SYSTEM

22. Within the UN system, special attention is being given to the critical need to improve co-ordination of environmental and sustainable development activities. The ILO has been actively supporting and participating in these efforts and the Governing Body has been kept closely informed of progress. For example, at the 241st Session (November 1988), the International Organisations Committee discussed the Oslo Conference on Sustainable Development and the work of the inter-agency group called the Designated Officials for Environmental Matters (DOEM).

23. The ILO has also been actively involved in the development of the System-Wide Medium-Term Environment Programme (SWMTEP), which is an ongoing process to facilitate improved planning and co-ordination within the UN system. The recently approved SWMTEP for the period 1990-95 contains over 50 specific references to possible action by the ILO, alone and in collaboration with others, concerning many different environmental issues, e.g. working environmental, rural development, housing, environmental training, industrial activities.

24. The ILO will continue to make every practicable effort to enhance the effectiveness of the co-ordination process within the UN system.

THE ILO AND THE ENVIRONMENT: PROSPECTS FOR THE FUTURE

25. Increasing interest and concern has been expressed by several ILO Industrial Committees and other meetings regarding the environment in 1988. For example, the Tenth Session of the Chemical Industries Committee adopted a resolution concerning the control and avoidance of toxic wastes; the 12th Session of the Metal Trades Committee adopted a resolution concerning the contribution of the

metal trades to the improvement of the environment and also proposed as one of its possible future agenda items "the contribution of the metal trades to the improvement of the environment and to the achievement of sustainable economic growth"; and the Committee on Conditions of Work in the Fishing Industry adopted a resolution on protection of the livelihood of fishermen, which refers in part to the importance of the protection of the marine environment and sound fish stock management. These examples provide an indication of the attention which environmental issues are receiving at the various meetings convened by the ILO. The reports prepared by the Office for such meetings are also giving increasing attention to the linkages between environmental problems and critical labour and social issues.

26. During the next biennium, there are a number of other issues which may require special attention by the ILO. One of the most important future environmental challenges may be that of "climatic change". Although the greatest attention is being devoted to the development of scientific and technical data and analyses of this phenomenon, there may be significant linkages between the possible effects of climatic change–or of policies and activities developed to delay or respond to climatic change–upon employment and social conditions. As a result, the ILO will need to monitor this issue closely in future. In addition, a large number of regional and international conferences are presently being scheduled between now and 1992. The ILO will need to carefully monitor the development of these conferences with a view to assessing at an early stage what contribution, if any, it should make within its very specific and limited areas of competence.

27. The ILO Programme and Budget proposals for 1990-91 have established environmental concerns and technological change as one of four priority themes for 1990-91. During the next biennium the ILO will concentrate its activities relating to this theme in the fields of employment promotion, training and the working environment, fields in which it has a clear mandate and unquestioned competence. When preparing those proposals, the Director-General expressed the conviction that the key test of whether the ILO would make progress towards environmentally sound and sustainable development would not be demonstrated only by the number of special items included in the draft proposals readily identifiable as "environmental projects" but rather, as stressed in the Brundtland Report, by the extent to which these considerations were more effectively integrated within all relevant ILO activities. In order to implement this integration strategy, a special unit concerning these issues has been established within the Office of the Assistant Director-General for Interdepartmental Programmes. In addition to providing staff resources to promote and support co-ordination and the development of specific efforts by technical departments to reflect these considerations more effectively in the implementation of their programmes, a limited amount of special additional resources

RESOLUTION CONCERNING THE CONTRIBUTION OF THE INTERNATIONAL LABOUR ORGANISATION TO THE PROTECTION AND ENHANCEMENT OF THE ENVIRONMENT RELATED TO WORK[1]

The General Conference of the International Labour Organisation,

Considering the ILO's solemn obligation "to further among the nations of the world programmes which will achieve . . . adequate protection for the life and health of workers in all occupations [and] the provision of adequate . . . housing and facilities for recreation and culture",

Noting with deep concern the increasing threat to the human environment and to the quality of human life, and aware of the specific problems to which this threat gives rise both in the advanced and in the developing countries,

Considering the harmful influence of nuclear weapons tests, especially those held in the atmosphere, upon the environment in which rural and urban workers conduct their activities,

Noting with concern occupational diseases and the large number of industrial accidents,

Recognising that economic and social development, vital to the achievement of the constitutional goals of the International Labour Organisation, and in particular to better working and living conditions, should not lead to a deterioration in the quality of human life, or in the environment in which human beings live and work,

Believing that the ILO has a special contribution to make to international, regional and national programmes for the protection and enhancement of the human environment, as the only organisation in which not only the governments, but also the employers and workers of the world are represented, and one with over have been provided to support those efforts. At the same time, RBTC resources will also be available to further support this integration strategy.

28. In addition to efforts under the regular budget, however, the Office will be seeking additional resources from multi-bilateral donors, as well as other funding sources. Already in 1988, the Government of Norway has approved a special project to support the ILO's special efforts towards sustainable development in advance of the Programme and Budget proposals for 1990-91. Priority will be given to the development of environmental components to be added to traditional ILO technical co-operation activities and the development of new activities in which the ILO may provide a unique comparative advantage.

29. The interdepartmental review of the Brundtland Report identified many other activities which the ILO might pursue in future to support environmentally sound and sustainable development. Nevertheless, recognising the important impact that the ILO's traditional activities have on the achievement of the ILO's fundamental objectives—which are themselves in direct support of sustainable development—the above-mentioned priorities and issues are considered the most important during the period of the Medium-Term Plan, 1990-95.

March 1989.

Notes

[1] See document GB.241/10/5/4 entitled Renewal of the Memorandum of Understanding on the International Programme on Chemical Safety (IPCS).

[2] For more detailed information on these training activities, see document GB.238/10/4/8 concerning Follow-up to UNEP's World Industry Conference on Environmental Management (1984).

half a century's experience in dealing with many of the problems raised by such programmes,

Believing, further, that the nature of that contribution is based on the ILO's constitutional responsibility for areas of social policy, and that the ILO's contribution will derive its usefulness from the influence which the concerted action of governments, employers and workers can exert for the protection of the human environment,

Considering that the working environment, in which countless men and women spend much of their daily lives, forms an important part of the human environment as a whole and that improvements in the working environment will consequently enhance the quality of the latter,

Considering that in many countries environmental pollution extends to residential areas and to areas for recreation and leisure activities,

Noting with satisfaction the ILO's past contribution to, and continuing emphasis on, improvements in the working environment under its standard-setting, technical co-operation, research, educational and information programmes in the field of occupational safety and health, aimed at the general humanisation of work,

Considering that the causes of the deterioration in conditions in the working environment are also among the main causes of the pollution of nature and are leading to a deterioration in the human environment,

Recognising that, in selecting techniques for industrialisation and for the mechanisation of agriculture, it is in the long-term interests of the developing countries to take account, as far as possible, of those techniques which, while being the most favourable to development, do not harm the environment,

Noting that many States have not ratified the Conventions relating to the various aspects of protection of the working environment, and that several member States have not ratified the Labour Inspection Convention, 1947 (No. 81), and the Labour Inspection (Agriculture) Convention, 1969 (No. 129),

Considering that government, labour and management should engage in a broader and more intensive dialogue on many of the issues raised by the enhancement of the human environment as a whole, and in particular on the consequences of environment policies for the security of employment and income, vocational training and retraining, labour mobility and management development,

Considering that measures taken at the national, regional and international levels to give effect to ILO principles and to the relevant international instruments would strengthen efforts to protect and enhance both the working and general environments,

Stressing the fact that economic development is a necessity for ensuring well-being in the developing countries, bearing it mind that it should take place in the context of general policies for conserving and enhancing both the working environment and the human environment;

1. Welcomes the initiative which led to the holding of the United Nations Conference on the Human Environment in Stockholm from 5 to 16 June 1972.

2. Calls upon member States to abstain from carrying out nuclear weapons tests, especially those which would be held in the atmosphere, in view of their harmful consequences in contaminating the rural and urban environments in which peasants and workers conduct their activities.

3. Pledges the full support and effective action of the International Labour Organisation to any concerted world campaign for the protection and enhancement of the human environment.

4. Emphasises the importance of the ILO's activities designed to enhance the environment related to work.

5. Calls upon governments and on employers' and workers' organisations–

(a) to intensify their efforts to promote improvements in the working environment;

(b) to co-operate closely in the formulation and implementation of comprehensive economic and social development policies which are designed to protect the human environment and to ensure the distribution and use of resources for the benefit of the community at large and the quality of life it enjoys; and

(c) to engage in close and regular consultation on any problems which such policies may raise and which may hamper the achievement of higher living standards in the community.

6. Calls particular attention to the following measures which member States should take into account in formulating the comprehensive economic and social development policies referred to in paragraph 5 *(b)* above:

(a) strengthening the labour inspection system and the imposition of adequate sanctions for offences of pollution and for the violation of safety and health standards;

(b) urban and industrial development which takes account of considerations relating to the development of the country and the environment as a whole;

(c) establishment of permissible levels for exposure of workers to harmful substances and by-products and definition of those levels after consultation with the organisations of workers and employers;

(d) vocational training and workers' education programmes designed to make the

individual worker more aware of the hazards of health which may arise in his working environment and instruct him in measures for his protection; and

(e) management development programmes designed to inform management of ways and means of ensuring improvements in the working environment, and protecting the human environment as a whole.

7. Reaffirms the responsibility of government and employers for taking protective and preventive measures in regard to their employees, and their duty to assure those concerned a real influence on the most suitable forms and methods of protection.

8. Urges member States to ratify and apply the Labour Inspection Convention, 1947 (No. 81), and the Labour Inspection (Agriculture) Convention, 1969 (No. 129), and other Conventions and Recommendations designed to protect the worker from occupational hazards and diseases.

9. Invites the Governing Body of the International Labour Office to instruct the Director-General—

(a) to pursue and expand research into new methods of protection and enhancement of the working environment in the different branches of the economy, particularly with regard to gas and vapours, noise and vibration, and radiation;

(b) to ensure that in the Programme of Industrial Activities prominence is given to new problems of the working environment arising in the different branches of the economy; and

(c) to study the problems arising in the field of working conditions and occupational safety and any relationship between the industrial accident rate and a deterioration in the working environment, and to prepare reports on the law and practice in each of these fields.

10. Invites the Governing Body of the International Labour Office, taking into account the reports thus prepared by the Office, to place on the agenda of a forthcoming session of the International Labour Conference the questions of occupational safety and the prevention of industrial accidents, as well as other questions related to the working environment, with a view to the possible adoption of new international instruments.

Note

[1] Adopted on 27 June 1972